Raise Your Credit Score

In 10 Easy Steps!

Angel Love, MBA, AFC®

From The Create Your Money Series

Dedication

This book is dedicated to the children... For my children and all of the other children that need to learn the lessons of managing money.

A very special Thank You to Mercedes, Paul, and Jason for being my children.

Thank You, Eddie and Allie my parents, for all of the lessons you taught me about managing money as a child.

Finally, Thank you Lord that I am yours... a child of God.

Acknowledgments

This 1st book in the Create Your Money Series *could not* have been possible without the help of my contributing team. Thank you Jason Watler, for designing the cover, Ihsaan "Cody" Singleton for photography, and several illustrators, editors, and researchers who worked anonymously on this project. Huge thanks to my dear friend, Nayanda Moore who stepped up and generously contributed her time to the task of editing. She didn't get to review the final edit so she's not to blame for any typos you might find. Kindly bring them to my attention for correction. I'm looking forward to working with the team of professionals gathered to help produce subsequent books in The Create Your Money Series.

I'm blessed with so many family members and friends who contributed to my growth as a financial professional, as well as to my personal development. My brothers, sister-friends, cousins, spiritual mentors, co-workers and people I've had the pleasure of knowing throughout the years. You are all too numerous to mention by name, but you know who are; you bring me joy.

Special thanks to Christina Stump for mentoring me when I was a financial intern in Colorado. Her passion for personal financial education impacted my approach to credit score management, and inspired me to encourage others in financial stewardship.

Extra special thanks to the men and women who serve in the United States Armed Forces, their spouses and family members. Thank you for sharing your lives with me, and for allowing me to be of service to you as a financial resource.

Table of Contents

Introduction

I am so excited to offer you 10 easy steps to improve your credit score. So many people struggle with bad credit and poor credit scores. Even those with good credit are finding it increasingly harder to be able to qualify for the things they want. Lenders, insurance company underwriters, cell phone providers, utility companies and employers all use credit scores and credit reports to help them make decisions about applicants. Even dating websites are encouraging people to provide their credit scores for potential matches to review and filter out those that don't have high credit scores! People know the importance of having a good credit score, but sometimes there's a lot of confusion around getting and keeping good credit.

The credit score is perceived as a number that reveals a person's level of financial risk and responsibility. Lenders look at the total amount of debt you can handle, relative to your income. They also review your credit report, employment history, assets and other factors before they decide if they will lend you money or not, but the credit score is a *huge* factor in this equation. There are things you can do to position yourself for more favorable credit terms *today*!

The higher your credit score, the lower your level of risk. The higher your credit score, the more competitive interest rates and terms you'll be offered because of your credit advantage. A high credit score can save you hundreds, or thousands of dollars over the life of any loans you get. Lower interest rates allow people to pay *less* for the money they borrow, and keep *more* money in their pocket. A high credit score can help increase your personal wealth overall.

A credit score is a three-digit number lenders use to determine the potential risk of lending you money. It is a dynamic number, changing according to what you pay off or charge up. Negative entries on your credit report such as collection accounts, can decrease your credit score by 50 points.

A public record can plummet your score by 75 points or more. Repossession, foreclosure, and bankruptcy can cost you 100-200 points! Once you discover the relationship between the financial actions you take and their impact on the credit score, you can make new decisions that change the direction of your credit score.

Out of all the subjects I cover as a Financial Counselor, the credit score and credit report are the most popular, yet most misunderstood topics. Recent studies have shown that Americans are more likely to discuss their salary, and weight, than to discuss their credit card debt, and credit scores. I wrote this book to help clear up some of the confusion with all of the misinformation out there. I want to help folks understand how to interpret their credit scores and present options to help them seriously improve their credit scores.

This is not a lengthy book that you'll have to spend the entire summer getting through. I've designed all of the books in The Create Your Money Series to be quick reads for those who want to review the information, take what they need and implement it immediately to get the results they want.

What qualifies me to talk to you about credit scores? I instinctively knew how to manage money from the time that I was a little kid. I had a paper route with my brother, and bagged groceries at the supermarket, sold gift cards, candy, and other novelties to develop a work ethic and a sense of entrepreneurship. Always fascinated with managing money, I knew by the time I graduated high school that I wanted to be a banker (or secretary...go figure). I started out on Wall Street and spent the first ten years of my career in administrative positions for a few banks and brokerage houses. I was fascinated with all things money; stocks, bonds, money transfers, gold and commodities, and I loved the thrill of the fast-paced, high-stakes financial environment

I was married to an Army man I met on Wall Street for 20 years, and traveled all around the country in support of my service-member. With a degree in psychology, I worked in various non-profit, social service agencies throughout the country for over 10 years. I gained valuable experience and a unique perspective during those years as a counselor and a military spouse. While helping others on their journeys of personal growth, many of those experiences contributed to my own personal development.

As a result of the financial decisions we made, my family's finances grew to six-figures and we lost it ... twice. I was always good with earning money but didn't always know how to keep it. I knew how to save to reach a particular goal but didn't always know how to make my money grow beyond that. I knew even less about managing credit or the relevance of a credit score. I started out with no credit history, built a high credit score and watched it plummet....twice. All of these personal financial crises and achievements taught me the hard way, valuable lessons about managing money and credit scores.

After several years of counseling others, I transferred my skills back to the business industry, working for investment firms. In 2009, I was awarded a FINRA Investor Foundation Fellowship with the chance to become an Accredited Financial Counselor® and I jumped at the opportunity. To me, financial counseling was the perfect "marriage" of my 10 years of business experience; combined with the 10 years I spent counseling others! Along the way I earned an MBA, and committed to helping people master their personal finances and maximize the money they make.

These past few years I've helped over 4,000 service members and their spouses access their credit scores and reports. Many of my clients chose to share their confidential reports with me during financial counseling sessions. I closely monitored the estimated value of certain actions consumers take on their credit reports and the impact those actions have in increasing or decreasing the credit score. I have learned proven tips that can help anyone improve their credit score and I'd like to share them with you.

The most common feedback I get after a financial planning counseling session is "No one *ever* told me this before." I wrote this book in an effort to make this information available to anyone who wants to improve his or her credit position. Others have referred to me as a "walking repository of financial information." I am fanatical about gathering the facts and making sense of them, but most of all I'm passionate about educating folks on personal financial management. Over the years I've learned that it doesn't matter how much money you make, or how much money you have.... it's what you *do* with what you *have*!

This book is the first in a series of financial books offering you quick and easy steps to get you up to speed on a variety of financial topics. This generation has been referred to as the fast food, microwave, and "give it to me quickly" generation! Social networks enable information to be disseminated globally in an instant. I want to make sure that the information you receive is timely and accurate, yet easy to implement immediately.

850

850 is the magic number. According to Fair, Isaac, & Company (FICO) 850 is the perfect credit score. FICO is the best known and most commonly used credit scoring model in the United States. Scores range from 300 to 850 and only 13% of the US population has a FICO credit score above 800. The highest credit scores are over 760, with half of the US population enjoying scores above 720.

There are many advantages to having a high credit score, including being offered the most competitive interest rates on homes, vehicles, and credit cards. People with high scores also pay lower premiums on the insurance policies they buy to protect those houses, and cars. There is a correlation between insurance risk and credit scores, so the score is a factor in determining the rates people pay for insurance policies. A high credit score can help a job applicant pass a background check more easily. Credit scores come from the information contained in credit reports. Job applicants sign forms authorizing potential employers to review their credit reports as part of the background check. If the information on the credit report is good, the applicant is thought to be financially responsible, so a high credit score can help secure promotions, bonuses, licenses, and security clearances as well.

People with low credit scores by contrast, are denied credit more often. A lower score limits the opportunities for competitive credit offers and makes you more susceptible to predatory lending. There is a whole market for sub-prime credit, defined as credit scores below 620. Applying the easy steps to increase your credit score can get you out of bad credit purgatory and put you in the position to earn more competitive interest rates. If you're already enjoying good credit, applying these steps can get you excellent credit and the most competitive offers on everything from mortgage interest rates to lucrative charge cards offering perks like frequent flyer miles.

Jewell P. was once the victim of a robbery and her purse was snatched. The thieves stole her identity to get goods and services in her name. After going through the ordeal of being a victim of a violent crime, Jewell had to painstakingly rebuild her credit history. Patient and resourceful, Jewell took the necessary steps to straighten out the mess. She worked hard to restore her credit score to the level she previously enjoyed. The nightmare of identity theft increased her sensitivity to guarding her personal information. Today, she is hyper-vigilant about monitoring her credit score and as a result is a member of the credit elite with a score of 815. Jewell, an African American woman, dispels the foolish idea that credit scores are somehow tied to race or gender and that the victim of identity theft has to suffer with a ruined credit score forever.

Ashley G. is the 21-year-old daughter of a military officer and his professional wife. Her parents instilled in her the importance of maintaining good credit and fiscal responsibility. They also "lent" her their credit history by making her an authorized user on one of their oldest, most valuable credit accounts. Ashley then got a credit card by herself without a co-signer and made sure she copied the credit behaviors of her parents, paying her balance down to zero every month. Ashley has an 805 Equifax FICO credit score, and an 807 on her TransUnion FICO. She defies conventional wisdom that you need to have several credit card accounts and a mortgage to get a credit score over 800.

I recently met with Charlene B. She and her husband are in the market for a $500,000 residential property in a metro area. She has held credit responsibly for over 20 years. A former military officer finishing her 2nd Master's degree with outstanding balances on her student loans while she is still in school ..... Charlene has one of the highest credit scores I've ever seen with an 834. Charlene proves that you don't need to have *everything* paid down to a zero balance in order to have a high credit score.

John P. is a married 56-year-old government worker from the Midwest. He still pays a mortgage on his 3,000 square-foot home, and has 8 credit cards. John keeps very low balances on these cards. He recently received a letter from a major credit reporting agency stating that his credit score ranks higher than 100% of US consumers. With 848 out of 850, John has one of the highest credit scores in the country.

This book is going to provide you with the information you need to improve your credit score so that you too can enjoy the benefits of having a high score. We'll review all aspects of a credit score, what it means, where it comes from and how it impacts the credit offers extended to you. I'm going to give you pointers that can be implemented *today* to increase your credit score. If you need to improve your cash flow before you can improve your credit score, you will find pointers on how to start

11

doing that as well. If you're already enjoying the benefits of a high credit score, you'll find valuable information on how to protect that score and maximize some of the perks that come along with having excellent credit.

Step 1: What is a Credit Score?

Credit scoring models are computerized and use analytics to evaluate information and produce a number that lenders and underwriters can use in their decision-making process. The score assesses how likely you are to either repay debt or be delinquent on your accounts. The information that produces a credit score comes from a consumer's credit report. It is statistically compared with millions of other people's information in the United States. The score is dynamic and will change according to actions you make as a consumer, such as paying off debt, or making new charges on a credit account.

Credit reporting agencies (CRAs) keep files on consumers containing information on your identity and employment. They report how well you've paid debts in the past, and which companies asked to review your credit file within the last two years. They also report any public record information that might be on file about you. Banks, credit unions, mortgage companies, department stores and other lenders send information about their customers to the CRAs each month. The agencies compile this information into a report, and memberships are sold to other merchants, employers, insurers, underwriters and businesses that have a legitimate purpose to see a credit report. The numbers are computed based on various factors, and the type of credit-scoring model used determines the output, your credit score.

There are three major CRAs in the United States: Equifax, TransUnion and Experian. The three CRAs compete with each other, and do not work together to share information about you (except under certain limited circumstances which we'll review later). Each agency is located in different regions of the country with Equifax headquartered in Atlanta, Georgia, TransUnion in Chicago, Illinois, and Experian (formerly known as TRW) located in Costa Mesa, California.

FICO partners with each of these agencies to evaluate the information on the credit reports and produces a separate credit score for each CRA. If your credit report were identical at all three CRAs then your credit score would also be the same at all three agencies, but that is never the case. Each of the CRAs collect different and sometimes conflicting information about you. Not all of your creditors choose to report to all three CRAs. Businesses have to pay for membership. Some creditors may report to just Equifax, and not to TransUnion or Experian. Other businesses may use TransUnion and exclude the others CRAs. This is why different credit reports will produce different credit scores. Sometimes, the scores are slightly different; sometimes, the numbers are so different, it's hard to believe that the reports are about the same person.

The FICO credit score range breaks down as follows:

- 760-850 – Excellent
- 700-759 – Very Good
- 660-699 – Good
- 620-659 – Fair
- 580-619 – Borderline
- 500 – 579 – Poor
- 300-499 – Unlikely to be approved

National Distribution of FICO Scores

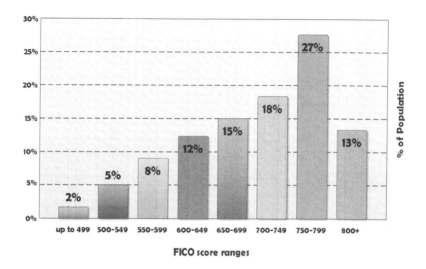

FICO score ranges

The graph above illustrates how FICO scores are distributed among the nation's population. If your score is 680, about 15% of the nation's population is in the same score range as you. A score of 720 puts you in the category with 18% of the population. Almost half of the nation's population has a score in the 700's. It used to be that a person with a score in the high 600's could get pretty good interest rates on things. Now you need to at least be in the low 700's to be offered competitive credit terms... 720 is the new 680.

Delinquency Rate By FICO Score

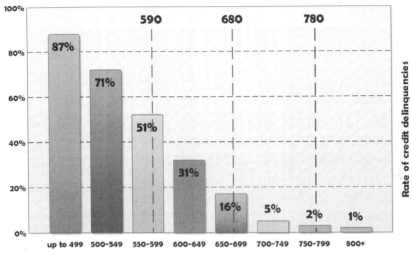

This graph shows how likely you are to be delinquent (or not) on a credit account according to your credit score. An account is considered delinquent when it is overdue, or paid more than 30 days late after the due date. Seriously delinquent is when an account is over 60 - 90 days late. The credit score predicts how likely you are to be seriously delinquent at least once, within the two years following the date the score was calculated. A person with a score of 590 will most likely be delinquent 51% of the time, within the next two years from the day the credit score was checked. A person with a 680 has a 15% chance of falling delinquent. Contrast this with a person whose credit score is 780, and expected to be delinquent only 2% of the time.

It is impossible for consumers to get the secret recipe for KFC Fried Chicken, McDonald's special sauce, Coca-Cola's formula, or Google's search algorithm. These proprietary formulas are heavily guarded secrets. In the same way, the *exact* formula for how FICO calculates its credit scores is also a closely guarded secret. We can *estimate* the weight of various factors as they relate to different actions and come up with an approximate value, but we cannot be *precise* because the scoring model is not made public.

The credit score itself used to be a closely guarded secret and lenders were prohibited from telling consumers what their credit score was. Most borrowers didn't even know such a thing even existed. It was thought that the scores were derived from such a complex mathematical model that the average consumer would have difficulty understanding the results. Legislation and progress changed all of that. Consumers now have the ability to access their credit reports, and credit scores and to receive interpretation. This impacts their use of credit, which directly impacts their credit score and affects their financial bottom line.

FICO owns their own scoring models and sells the use of it to other businesses. 90% of lenders and underwriters use FICO. Other scoring models have been produced to compete, but FICO is still the dominant market leader. The other credit scoring models use their own formulas to calculate their credit scores. They may have different score ranges, but all of them are basically designed to translate your credit history into a credit score. FICO customizes a different credit-scoring model for each of the three major CRAs, which can get a little confusing:

- A FICO Beacon® score is used with Equifax
- Experian/Fair Issac Risk Model is used with Experian
- EMPIRICA®/ Classic is used with TransUnion

On top of that, each of the CRAs produce their *own* score in-house, which they then sell on their own websites and offer other services such as credit-monitoring:

- Equifax owns ScorePower
- Experian has PLUS score
- TransUnion has TransScore and TrueCredit.

To further add to the credit score confusion, all three CRAs joined forces to develop the VantageScore, which was launched in 2006. If that's not a dizzying array of credit scoring models, you should know that lenders sometimes use their *own* in-house credit-scoring model, along with the FICO score to make risk decisions about you. You might want to ask a lender/underwriter which credit scoring model is being used to assess your level of risk. Keep in mind that 90% of lenders use the FICO score so it is the one to watch.

The differences between the various credit scores should be around 10-20 points, but sometimes the discrepancies can be as wide as 50 -70 points so it's important that you check your scores and reports with each CRA. The differences in the credit score are due to differences in the information contained in the credit reports and the weight assigned to the values. Negative information might be on one credit report, but not another. Keep in mind the agencies don't share information with each other, and not all creditors report consumer information to all three credit reporting agencies.

When the VantageScore was introduced in 2006 it was meant to be serious competition for the FICO score. While FICO has been the dominant credit-scoring model, VantageScore reports an increase in customers for their score. According to their website, seven of the top 10 financial institutions are using VantageScore along with 6 of the top 10 credit card issuers, 4 of the top auto lenders, and 4 out of 5 of the leading mortgage lenders. It is unclear if the lenders are using both the VantageScore and FICO, or either one exclusively. It's not a bad idea to ask your lenders, which credit scoring model they use. Consumers don't get to choose which score a lender uses.

The advantage of the Vantage score is that it allows what is known as "thin file" consumers (folks with little to no credit history) to get a credit score. Young adults just beginning their career, people who have recently been divorced and have no credit in their name, recent immigrants, and those that have been through bankruptcy are considered "thin file" consumers.

VantageScore currently has a score range of 501-990. The numerical values are assigned a letter grade along five tiers, with "A" grades being considered the least risky by a lender:

- A: 900–990
- B: 800–899
- C: 700–799
- D: 600–699
- F: 501–599

Both TransUnion and Experian sell Vantage credit scores directly to consumers on their websites. TransUnion also offers a TransRisk and/or a Vantage credit score for free through their CreditKarma website. CreditSesame offers free credit scores through its website. They use Experian's National Equivalency Score, which ranges from 360-840. Experian also uses PlusScore, which is primarily an education model and is typically not used by lenders; it allows you to monitor changes in your credit score. FICO scores are sold through the MyFico website (read further for links).

When you visit the CRA websites, you'll be offered either a single credit score, or a combination of all three credit scores. The CRAs usually encourage you to subscribe to some sort of credit monitoring service that may include identity theft protection. They offer interactive score estimators that show the impact of specific actions and how those actions affect your credit score. Most of these websites also offer free educational resources on how to improve your credit score.

Watch out for the flashy ads that offer you a "free credit score". If you visit these websites, be sure you read the fine print because many people find out the hard way that these "free credit scores" are not *free* at all. These websites may offer a score that has nothing to do with FICO, or VantageScore. They often require you to sign up with a credit card that will automatically debit your account for monthly services (score updates and other reports that are emailed to you). The scores may be based on their own in-house calculations, and not based

19

on any information provided by the three major CRAs. These types of scores are jokingly referred to as FAKO scores, and may have little to no resemblance to any credit score used by an actual lender. I'll provide links up ahead to help you access some CRA credit scores for free.

Each of the CRAs produce their own scores and the exact details of how the credit scores are calculated are unknown. The published score ranges are as follows:

- Equifax PowerScore: 300-850
- Experian/PlusScore/National Equivalency Score: 330-830
- TransUnion TransRisk Score: 300-850
- Vantage Score: 501-990 (assigned a letter grade, A-F)

VantageScore recently announced it was releasing a new credit-scoring model that would match FICO's 300-850 range. This latest version has the potential to provide credit scores for 30 million consumers who were previously considered "unable to be scored". Most credit scoring models call for at least 6 months recent activity in order to generate a score. The new changes could boost scores for many credit applicants and help those who have little to no credit history, or no recent credit activity on their reports. The new VantageScore will factor in rent and utility payment records (if those providers choose to report), providing a boost to those with little to no credit history.

Currently, accounts that go into collections are factored into the credit score for up to 7 years. It doesn't matter if those debts are paid off, or still outstanding the impact to the score is still calculated with the most damage occurring within the first two years. The new Vantage scoring model will not calculate debt that was paid in full or settled, as long as there is a zero balance. Special consideration will be given to victims of natural disasters, and they will be protected against negative accounts often occurring in the financial aftermath of such disasters.

FICO is also reviewing new ways to calculate information for those with little to no credit history.

Notes/Action Plan

Notes/Action Plan

Step 2: How is Your Credit Score Calculated?

In order to improve your credit score it's important that you understand how your credit score is calculated. Credit scores change according to what you just paid off, charged up, or what information has been corrected, updated, or removed from your credit report. First we'll review the factors that make up your FICO credit score, and then we'll review some pointers to start improving your credit score today. Other credit scoring models (such as VantageScore) may consider similar factors with slight differences in the weight assigned to each value.

The composition of the average FICO score is:

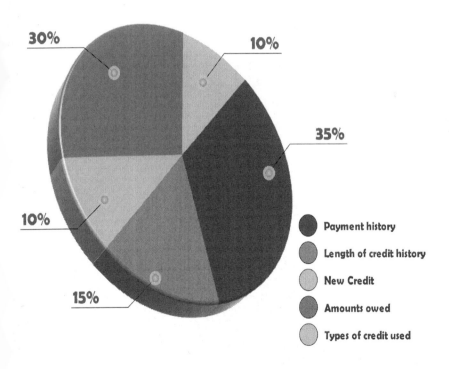

Let's take an individual look at each piece of the credit score pie:

Payment History:

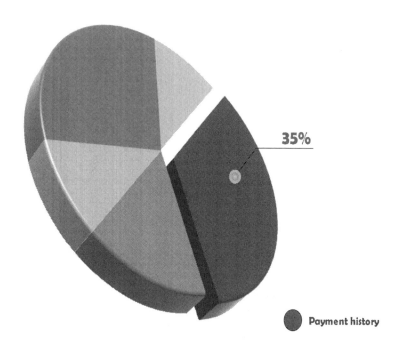

35%

● Payment history

       Your payment history is 35% of your FICO credit score. It's the most important part of your credit score and lenders look at this piece first. This includes information on how well you've handled credit in the past. Payment history reflects how you paid your mortgages, car loans, credit cards, retail cards, student loans and bank loans in the past, with the most recent activity carrying the most weight. Your lenders send payment information about your accounts to the credit reporting agencies on a regular basis, typically monthly. They report whether or not you pay your bills on time, if you've missed payments, or if accounts are delinquent (30, 60, 90 days past due).

Accounts that end up in the courthouse such as bankruptcy, court-ordered judgments in favor of your creditors and tax liens are also included here. This information is public record and credit reporting agencies (CRAs) send people to the courthouse to scour the records and collect the information which is then added to your credit report. Public record accounts are the most damaging to your credit score. Delinquent accounts that have been charged-off, and/or placed with collections are also noted under payment history, along with delinquent accounts that have been paid off by the consumer. Payment history problems have their most severe impact within the first two years and become less important as time goes on.

Amounts Owed:

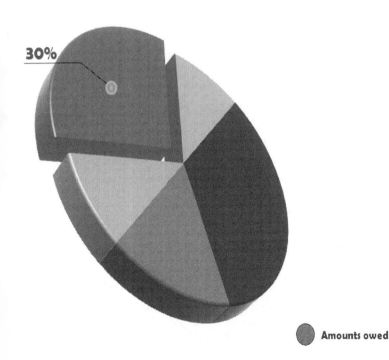

Amounts owed

30% of the credit score is the amount owed on each credit account and this is the 2nd largest part of your credit score. This includes the number of accounts you owe money on, and the balance due on each type of account you have (revolving, installment, and mortgage accounts). The amount of revolving credit you have available to use and how much of that credit you actually use is your credit utilization, and it is one of the most important factors in this category. Also included is the amount of debt left on installment loans such as mortgages, cars, and student loans.

Length of Credit History:

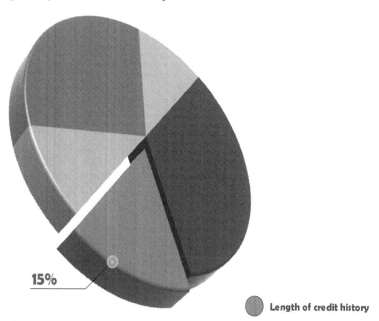

15%

● Length of credit history

Credit History is 15% of the credit score and includes information on how long you've held your various accounts. All of your open accounts are counted here. It doesn't matter if the payment history is positive or negative on them, if the account is still open it's included here. Negative account history can be removed after 7 years and won't be reported here after that time. Positive accounts that are now closed, and were in good standing can be reported indefinitely which is to your advantage. It doesn't matter if the consumer closed the account or if the lender closed it. These old accounts with good history benefit consumers because you accumulate more points for demonstrating that you've been responsible with credit for longer periods of time. When you last used the accounts is also a factor in the length of credit history.

New Credit:

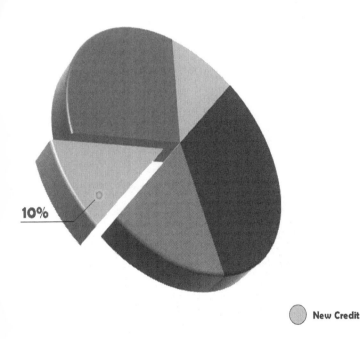

New Credit

New Credit is 10% of the credit score and includes the number of new accounts recently opened. Any time you fill out an application for new credit or authorize someone to check your credit report to determine if they will lend you money, it is a hard inquiry. The number of hard credit inquiries you have, as well as when the last hard credit inquiry occurred is considered.

Typically the activity within the last two years is noted, with the hard inquiries of the past year having the most impact. If you open a new account after a hard inquiry, that action is counted as well. New accounts can impact you depending upon your credit utilization, and the overall age of your other accounts, as well as other factors.

Types of Credit Used:

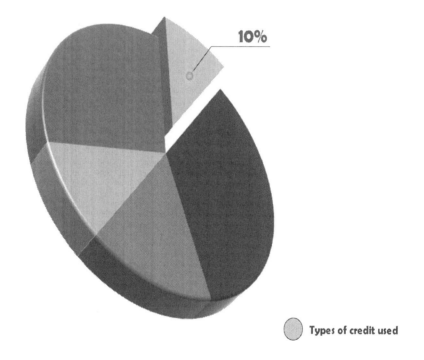

10%

Types of credit used

Lenders consider the different types of credit you use responsibly, which accounts for 10% of your credit score. The three types of credit are mortgage, installment and revolving credit. Installment loans allow borrowers to repay both the principal and interest in equal installments. Student loans and car loans are examples of installment credit. Primary mortgages are typically installment loans (such as a 30-year fixed) but mortgage credit could also be revolving (such as home equity line of credit). Both mortgages and other installment loans are considered closed-end, when the payments are complete the loan is closed. Revolving credit is a type of open-ended account where the line of credit remains available to the borrower to use over and over again. Credit cards are revolving credit accounts.

Debt can be secured or unsecured. Secured credit is backed by collateral such as a car, house, or boat. If the borrower defaults the lender repossesses the collateral. Unsecured credit may be granted on the basis of your credit score and income. Signature loans from the bank and most revolving credit cards are unsecured. If the borrower defaults the lender might choose to charge off the debt, and sell it to a collection agency. The different types of credit grantors used are factored here as well. Getting credit from a major bank or credit union is different than getting credit from a department store, which is different than getting credit from a finance company.

What Is Not Included in Your Credit Score?

In the past, certain groups of people have had difficulty getting competitive credit offers. They were unfairly assessed on factors that had nothing to do with their level of credit risk, such as ethnicity, religion, skin color, or marital status. The advantage of using a credit score is that it allows consumers to be assessed on factors directly related to their credit risk. A computer does the scoring and a computer obtains the results. The use of credit score in the decision-making process eliminates people's personal biases and opinions. That said, there are some things that do not affect your credit score:

- Ethnicity, race, or religion.
- Age, gender
- Marital status
- Income, occupation, employment history

- Interest rates you currently pay
- Length of time at your current address
- Whether or not you own or rent your home
- The use of credit counseling services
- Checking your credit yourself

Some of these issues are illegal for a lender to use in assessing applicants for credit. Under the Consumer Credit Protection Act, a lender may not use race, color, religion, national origin, sex, marital status, or receipt of public assistance, when evaluating an applicant for credit. A lender will use some of the *other* factors, such as type of employment, when deciding if they will lend you money, but that information is not computed in the credit score. A lender will also want to know how much you make before lending to you, but your salary is not included in your credit report or score. A lender can use whether or not you own or rent your home as an indication of your assets, but that's not included in computing the credit score. How much you make and how much you own is not a predictive factor of whether or not you'll pay your bills on time.

Child support obligations can be included on a credit report and factored into a credit score especially if the child support payments are in arrears. Making regular child support payments won't necessarily improve your credit score, but failing to make child support payments will hurt your score. While on-time payments aren't usually reported to the CRA, missed payments can be reported. If you have a history of missing payments and a government agency wins a judgment against you for child support, it will end up on your credit report. This can damage your score by 20-50 points or more. Federal law mandates that the name of the non-custodial parent and their child support payment history is periodically reported to the CRAs. How and when that information gets reported varies from state to state.

Understand the Risk Reason Codes

It's helpful to know the specific reason codes lenders/underwriters use when scoring applicants. The various credit-scoring models use different risk factors, or risk score reason codes to evaluate applicants for credit. Each risk code has a corresponding reason statement. Risk codes are used to convert your credit risk into a numerical value (the score). If you've ever received a declination letter from a creditor, it will usually contain the abbreviated version of a risk code. Risk codes don't tell you exactly how many points you lose for specific reasons, but they can be used to figure out the areas where your credit score may be challenged.

Risk reason codes can also be used as a tool for maintaining good credit. Model the codes that keep your scores high and avoid those that lower your score. If an action is not on the list (such as when an account is closed by the lender) it's probably because that action has no impact on your credit score. If there is negative information on your credit report when a lender pulls it, a declination letter will reveal the top four reason codes the lender based his/her decision on. The codes will be listed in the order of importance. This is helpful in determining which areas to focus on the most as you improve your credit score.

The FICO risk reason codes are far too numerous to list them all here. Additionally, other credit scoring models use their own reason codes. The following list is a small sampling of risk score reason codes:

- Account payment history is too new to rate
- Amounts owed on accounts is too high
- Amounts owed on delinquent accounts
- Amounts owed on revolving accounts is too high
- Amount past due on accounts
- Date of last inquiry too recent
- Derogatory public record or collection filed

- Level of delinquency on accounts
- Serious delinquency
- Serious delinquency, and public record or collection filed
- Serious delinquency, derogatory public record, or collection filed
- Lack of recent auto finance loan information
- Lack of recent bank/national revolving information
- Lack of recent consumer finance company account information
- Lack of recent installment loan information
- Lack of recent revolving account information
- Level of delinquency on accounts
- No recent non-mortgage balance information
- No recent revolving balances
- Length of time accounts have been established
- Length of time installment loans have been established
- Length of time revolving accounts have been established
- Time since delinquency is too recent or unknown
- Time since derogatory public record or collection is too short
- Time since most recent account opening is too short
- Number of accounts with delinquency
- Number of bank/national revolving accounts with balances
- Number of established accounts
- Proportion of balances to credit limits on bank/national revolving or other revolving accounts is too high
- Proportion of loan balances to loan amounts is too high
- Serious delinquency, derogatory public record or collection filed
- Too few accounts currently paid as agreed
- Too few accounts with recent payment information
- Too many accounts recently opened
- Too many accounts with balances
- Too many bank or national revolving accounts
- Too many consumer finance company accounts

- Too many inquiries last 12 months

As you continue to read you'll discover some strategies you can take if your credit score is challenged by any of the risk reason codes and corresponding statements.

Notes/Action Plan

_____
_____
_____
_____
_____
_____
_____
_____
_____
_____
_____
_____
_____
_____
_____
_____
_____
_____
_____
_____
_____
_____
_____
_____
_____
_____
_____
_____
_____
_____
_____

Notes/Action Plan

Step 3: Assess Your Credit Position

Now that you know where credit scores come from and how they are calculated let's talk about what you need to do to improve the credit score. What's your motivation for improving your credit score and what's the credit score you'd like to achieve? Identifying the reasons why you want to improve your credit score helps determine the direction you take. It directly impacts your level of commitment to the task. Someone who only wants a higher credit score so that they can qualify for a house or a car and buy more things is going to approach this a lot differently than someone who genuinely wants to improve their financial situation overall. If you want to learn better money management skills, and master your credit position I will give you tips that you can implement, but you must be willing to put in the work in order to get the results you can be proud of.

In order to repair your credit you need to first assess your credit position. The easiest way to do this is to pull your credit report from each of the three major credit-reporting agencies (CRAs). Check your credit score and review the information that is being reported about you. Don't be afraid to check this information out. It's better to know where you stand and be in a position to improve it, than to not know at all. Don't worry about lowering your score if you check your own credit report. Checking your credit yourself is *always* a soft inquiry and will not impact your score at all. In fact, you can check your credit report 5 times a day; every day... and it won't impact your score one bit.

The Federal Trade Commission (FTC) is the nation's consumer protection agency and enforces the Fair Credit Reporting Act (FCRA). The FCRA is a law which protects the rights of consumers by promoting the accuracy, fairness, and privacy of the information contained in your credit reports.

Under FCRA you have the right to know what's in your credit report, and who requested to see your credit report within the last two years.

Every citizen of the United States is entitled to a free copy of their credit report from each of the three major CRAs once per year. If you're unemployed, looking for work, receiving public assistance, or a victim of identity theft you are also entitled to a free copy of your credit report from each of the three major CRAs as these life events occur. Under federal law you're also entitled to a free credit report if a company takes any adverse action against you. This means that if you are denied credit, insurance, or a job based on the information contained in your credit report, the company has to send you a letter stating so. You have 60 days after receiving this notice to request a copy of the credit report.

The Free File Disclosure Rule of the Fair and Accurate Credit Transactions Act (FACT Act) requires Equifax, Experian and TransUnion to give you a free copy of your credit report every 12 months, but you have to ask for it. The three CRAs collaborate to operate a website, provide an 800 number, and an address for consumers to use in order to access their credit reports for free. www.annulcreditreport.com is the only website authorized to give you a free copy of your credit report from each of the three major credit-reporting agencies, under federal law. Pull your credit report *today* and see what's on there... don't delay!

There are a lot of copycat websites that claim to offer, "free credit reports" and you should avoid these websites if all you want is your free credit report. These websites have nothing to do with the authorized free program, and usually require that you use a credit card to sign up for some sort of monthly subscription or credit-monitoring service. Some of them allow you to access the product during a free trial period and then charge your credit card if you don't cancel before the trail period ends. These websites are !egitimate in that they offer you a credit report and score, but it is *not* the free authorized website that provides the full credit reports from the three major CRAs per FACT.

Go to www.annualcreditreport.com and use the bank-level encrypted website to order your credit report from each agency. After you pull a report from one agency it will automatically transfer you over to the next agency. You can view your reports, save them as a .pdf file to your desktop and print them out. You have about 30 days to access the reports after you pull them. You will be eligible to receive another free report 12 months from the date that you last pulled your credit reports. Once you've checked your credit and have begun to do the work to repair it, you can pull subsequent credit reports on a quarterly basis. Pull your Equifax report in January, Experian in May and TransUnion in September. By staggering your pulls quarterly you can monitor your own credit throughout the year for free.

The toll-free telephone number to order your free annual credit report is 877-322-8228. If you prefer to mail in your request, go to:

www.ftc.gov/bcp/edu/resources/forms/requestformfinal.pdf and download the Annual Credit Report Request Form. Mail the completed version to:

Annual Credit Report Request Service
P.O. Box 105281
Atlanta, GA 30348-5281

In addition to the Federal Law, there are state laws that provide their residents a free copy of the credit report each year. If you live in any of the following states you can get an *additional* free report once a year *directly* from the credit bureaus:

- Colorado – one free report every 12 months, $8 afterwards
- Georgia – free
- Maine – one free report every 12 months, $5 afterwards
- Maryland – one free report every 12 months

- Massachusetts – one free report every 12 months
- New Jersey – one free report every 12 months
- Vermont – one free report every 12 months
- Puerto Rico – free

State law provides reduced fee credit reports for residents of the following areas:

- California - $8
- Connecticut - $5 initially - $7.50 afterwards
- Minnesota - $3
- Montana - $8.50
- The Virgin Islands - $1

I'm including a sample of the type of letter that you'd send to the credit reporting agencies to request your free credit report per state law. Send your request for a free or reduced price credit report per state law to:

Equifax Credit Information Services, Inc.
P.O. Box 740241
Atlanta, GA 30374

TransUnion LLC
Consumer Disclosure Center
P.O. Box 1000
Chester, PA 19022

Experian
National Consumer Assistance Center
P.O. Box 2002
Allen, Texas 75013

Your Name
Address
City, State, Zip Code

Date

Name of Credit Reporting Agency
Address
City, State, Zip Code

To Whom It May Concern:

I am sending this letter to request a copy of my credit report in accordance with the law in the state of _____.

To expedite my request, I am including my personal information:

Full name:

Social Security #:

Date of Birth:

Full address:

Home telephone #:

Enclosed please find my payment of (amount if any to cover the cost of the report).

Thank you for your prompt attention to this matter.

Sincerely,

Your Name

The free and/or reduced price credit reports you receive per state law do not count against your free annual report at www.annualcreditreport.com. You can still access that website for free once per year like everyone else, and if you stagger those pulls while accessing your free state reports you could potentially pull a free credit report every 2 months or so. Residents of the states that allow for an additional annual free credit report need to apply directly to the CRA to exercise that right:

Equifax	1-800-685-1111	www.equifax.com
Experian	1-888-397-3742	www.experian.com
TransUnion	1-800-888-4213	www.transunion.com

The credit reports are free but they sell you the credit scores. You can purchase a FICO score at:

www.myfico.com/Guest_Home.aspx. There are usually special offers to get a free score if you join one of their credit monitoring services, otherwise the scores cost around $20 each. Type "coupon codes FICO credit scores" into your search engine and you should see a link to the website www.retailmenot.com, which offers coupon codes for many different products and services purchased online. You may be able to buy the score at 50% off by using one of their coupon codes.

For a free credit score go to: www.creditkarma.com. Credit Karma is powered by TransUnion and offers a free Vantage score and free credit monitoring with real-time notifications if there are any changes to your credit accounts. Experian offers a similar service through:

www.creditsesame.com. You can get a free Experian credit score, and use their credit tools to help you improve your score. Both websites allow you to sign up for free, no credit card required. If you are a Military Service Member on Active-duty you can always get a free FICO score from your Personal Financial Manager on your nearest military installation.

FINRA is the Financial Industry's Regulating Agency. The FINRA Investor Education Foundation and SaveAndInvest.org have partnered together to provide Active-duty military service members and their spouses with free FICO scores. Contact a Personal Financial Manager (PFM) or a FINRA Fellow Accredited Financial Counselor on most military installations for more information. Active-Duty service-members have earned the privilege to get professional help with credit score/credit report management at no cost.

While you are checking your status with the three major CRAs there are two other agencies you might be interested in checking as well. Lexis-Nexis, and Innovis, are not as widely known as the three major CRAs but one is a major compiler of private intelligence information, and the other is considered the "4th credit bureau".

LexisNexis compiles personal information on citizens. Choicepoint was the premier private intelligence agency until 2008 when LexisNexis brought them out. Employers and landlords use this information to screen you and assess your suitability as an employee or tenant. Underwriters and lenders may use this report in conjunction with other reports to make decisions about you. Insurance companies also use this information in evaluating you for auto or property insurance. LexisNexis is subject to FACT Act and is obligated to provide consumers with a full file disclosure report once every 12 months if you request it. Pull this report, and check it for accuracy. For instructions on how to access your LexisNexis full file disclosure go to the website at:

https://personalreports.lexisnexis.com/

You'll receive directions on downloading the official request form and a list of the types of identification to include with you request. Mail your completed form and copies of identification to:

LexisNexis Consumer Center
Attn: Full File Disclosure
P.O. Box 105108
Atlanta, GA 30348-5108

LexisNexis also provides a free insurance report called the C.L.U.E. in compliance with the FACT act. The C.L.U.E. contains a detailed seven-year history of losses related to your personal property and insurance providers review this information. If you haven't filed a claim against your auto or property insurance in the last seven years there will probably not be a recent report for you. Access this report through: https://personalreports.lexisnexis.com/fact_act_claims_bundle/landing.jsp

The website is user friendly and there are sample reports, as well as instructions on how to read the reports. Please note there is a separate C.L.U.E. report for both personal property and auto reports. You should review this information and be certain it is accurate. The premiums you pay on your insurance policies may be tied to information contained in this report. You have a right to dispute any information you believe is inaccurate. The LexisNexis website instructs you on how to file a dispute.

LexisNexis is not a credit-reporting agency and does not keep credit reports or credit scores. LexisNexis says that it does not collect any healthcare or medical record information on citizens, nor does it collect bank information. All of the information in their files can be reviewed through the full disclosure report and the insurance report, which you can access for free. LexisNexis also has the following types of reports available for a small fee:

- Home Seller's Disclosure Report
- Insurance and Credit Reports
- Vital Records (birth, death, marriage and divorce certificates)
- Health Care Credentials Check

- Lawsuits, Liens, and Judgments Business Check

There is a link to the First Advantage website for any employment history and residential information that may have been collected about you.

While Lexis-Nexis is not a CRA, Innovis, based in Philadelphia, Pennsylvania, is considered the "4th CRA in the US". A small number of lenders and banks buying consumer credit reports use them. Mortgage holder GMAC, and communications giant Verizon are Innovis customers, so the contents of this report may be worth checking out. Fannie Mae and Freddie Mac require organizations that partner with them to report to Innovis, so you may find a lot of mortgage information being reported here. You can order a free copy of your Innovis report every 12 months, dispute information, and have the reported corrected, just as you can with any other credit report. It does not appear that the agency produces a credit score on consumers.

Complete a request for your Innovis credit report online by going to: https://www.innovis.com/InnovisWeb/

To order the report by phone call: 1-800-540-2505. The report will be mailed to you within 3-5 business days after your request.

To order by mail go online to download the Innovis credit report request form and mail the completed forms with the acceptable forms of identification to:

Innovis
Attn: Consumer Assistance
P.O. Box 1689
Pittsburgh, PA 15230-1689

Notes/Action Plan

Notes/Action Plan

Step 4: Dispute Inaccurate Information on Your Credit Report

Now that you've reviewed the information on your credit report let's focus on what to do to improve it. Under the Fair Credit Reporting Act, the accuracy of the information on your credit report is the responsibility of the credit reporting agency (CRA) and the creditor that reported the information about you to the CRA. If the information is inaccurate or incomplete you have a right to have that information updated.

Studies have shown that as many as 80% of credit reports contain errors so it's important that you check your report carefully. These errors cost consumers money by causing them to pay higher interest rates, and incur additional charges and fees for goods and services. To dispute inaccurate information, notify the CRA in writing, or initiate an on-line dispute. CRAs have at least 30 days from the date that you dispute an item to investigate.

During the dispute resolution process, the CRA notifies the information provider that the item is being disputed. The lender has to verify the accuracy of that item and report back to the CRA. Whether or not the information is removed while being disputed depends on the practices of the CRA. If the information is inaccurate or can't be verified, it must be updated or deleted. The investigation process can take 30-45 days. When it's complete the CRA will provide you with the written results either on line or via mail (whichever way you initiated the dispute).

You're entitled to another free copy of your credit report if the dispute results in a change to your credit report. Request that any creditors who reviewed your report while the inaccurate information was still on there, be given an updated copy of your report.

There are many types of errors found on the average credit report. Personal information such as your name, address, date of birth, and social security number can all be inaccurate. While these items may not impact your credit score they can make you more susceptible to identity theft. Minimize that risk by making sure your vital information is accurate. Correct such things as the misspelling of your name, and the listing of the wrong generation (Jr., Sr., II). Check to see if your current spouse's name is correct, your former spouses name is removed, and that the DOB is yours.

Verify that the addresses listed are places you actually lived in years past. If you've ever paid a bill, or opened a new account from a temporary location that address might be listed on your credit report as well. It's not uncommon to find the address of hotels, jobs, colleges, and relatives you temporarily lived with on your credit report. If you ever received mail, paid bills, or opened new accounts from that location it was reported to the CRA. Divorced couples may find that the new address of their former spouse is listed on their own credit report, even if they never lived at that address. If there are jointly held accounts still open and the bills go to the former spouse at the new address, it may appear on your credit report because it's listed as the billing address. Be sure to dispute any addresses that you don't recognize to minimize exposure to identity theft.

Some credit reports list mortgages or other loans twice, and accounts that don't belong to the consumer at all. Some reports don't contain positive information that should be included in the report. For example, one of your creditors may list the name, address, and credit limits, without actually listing your good payment history on that account. You don't get to determine which CRA your lender chooses to report too, but you can request that positive missing information is included if a creditor already reports to a specific CRA. Dispute these types of errors online or send letters requesting correction, updating or deletion. A sample letter to dispute inaccurate information follows:

Your Name
Address
City, State, Zip Code

Date

Name of Credit Reporting Agency
Address
City, State, Zip Code

To Whom It May Concern:

I am writing to request that you remove inaccurate information from my credit report. This inaccurate information is impacting my ability to get loans at the more competitive interest rates. I am including proof of the correct items if you need to verify them prior to removing the inaccurate information.

I am asking you to make the changes within 30 days in accordance to the Fair Credit Reporting Act. Please send me a copy my updated credit report with the corrected information as soon as the changes are completed.

Sincerely,

Your Name

You have the right to request copies of any correspondence between the CRA and the creditor used during the dispute resolution/verification process. If the information provider gave the CRA copies of any bills, or original credit agreements you might have signed, you have the right to request to review that as well.

Sometimes an investigation doesn't resolve the dispute with the credit-reporting agency. If that becomes the case, you're allowed to put 100-word statement on that specific account with your version of the events. This statement will be included in future credit reports. Some CRAs will allow you to upload a statement online; others want you to send the statement in writing.

A sample letter to the CRA requesting a dispute and investigation might look this:

Your Name
Address
City, State, Zip Code

Date

Name of Credit Reporting Agency
Address
City, State, Zip Code

Attn: Dispute Resolution/Complaint Department

Dear Sir or Madam:

I am writing to dispute the following information contained in my credit report (number of credit report if you have it). I am attaching a copy of the credit report and have highlighted the items I am disputing.

I am disputing the following items (list item by name of creditor, account number, court ID number and type of credit account) because this information is (inaccurate, incomplete, outdated). Describe why the item is inaccurate, incomplete, or outdated. I am requesting that this item be deleted, updated, corrected and that my credit report be updated.

I am enclosing a copy of (the paid bill, court records, or other supporting information). Please reinvestigate this item, and correct the disputed item(s) as soon as possible.

Sincerely,

Your Name
Enclosures: (List whatever you are enclosing)

Notes/Action Plan

Notes/Action Plan

Step 5: Raise Your Score by Managing Each Piece of the Credit Score Pie

Raise your Credit Score by Managing Your Payment History

A huge part of raising your credit score involves taking a hard look at the specific factors of your credit score, and implementing strategies for each one. Even if you're doing most of the right things to manage a good credit score, you could be overlooking specific strategies that raise your score from good to excellent.

Review your credit report, paying close attention to the payment history on each individual account to ensure that payments are being reported on time. On-time payments are crucial in managing your credit and account for more than 35% of the score. One of the most important things you can do to improve your credit score *today* is *never* pay a bill more than 30 days late. How much a 30-day late payment impacts your credit score depends on various factors within the scoring model. While a 30-day late payment can decrease an average score by 30 points, a person with a higher credit score (780 for example) can lose up to 90 points just for paying the bill 30 days late. Higher credit scores stand to lose more points for negative actions than lower credit scores.

If the bill is due on the 7th of the month, make sure the bill is paid on or before the 7th. The lender has the right to report the account late the 1st day the bill is past due, but they typically don't report the account late to the credit reporting agency (CRA) until it is 30 days past due. If you have to pay that bill on the 29th day after the due date, you might be okay. Depending upon when the payment posts and the lenders late policy, you'll still be charged a late fee, but at least you'll avoid a 30 day late report. Do everything in your power to avoid paying the bill 30 days past due.

It's easy to overlook bills with the avalanche of junk mail and email most people find in their mailboxes these days. Unfortunately, missing payment due dates cost more in the long run with added late fees, interest rate increases, and as interest continues to accrue on the accounts. The higher your credit score, the more points you stand to lose through actions like a late payment. Put your bills on a payment schedule and use options like automatic billing and auto-pay to reduce late payments. If you generally pay your bills on-time and have one 30-day late payment you can ask your creditor to remove the blemish as a courtesy to you and reverse any late-fees. Whether or not they do it will depend on their policy and your payment history with them.

Negative information that is accurate can stay on the credit report for 7-10 years. Everyone is entitled to a fresh start however, and adverse information should be removed from the credit report after 7 years. A bankruptcy can stay on the report for up to 10 years before it is removed. Unpaid judgments can stay on the credit report for 7 years or until the statute of limitations runs out, whichever is longer.

Accurate bad payment history generally stays on the credit report for 7 years, but you might not have to wait that long for it to be removed. We'll talk more about that when we review settling debts. Some CRAs make it easy for consumers to figure out when the 7-year time period ends. They note adverse information as "scheduled to be removed" and tell you the month and year when the 7-year period ends. For CRAs that don't annotate this information, use the "date of last activity" or the "last reporting date" on the account and calculate 7 years from that date to estimate when the account is eligible for removal. Accounts should drop off automatically by computer. However, it is your responsibility to check and review the accuracy of the credit report to make sure that outdated adverse accounts are removed.

Good accounts with positive information can stay on the credit report indefinitely, and actually contribute to an increased credit score. Your oldest revolving credit account being "paid as agreed" is probably one of your strongest accounts. If the account is still open you might want to leave it open, even if you don't use it. This account "ages or dates" you, it tells a lender that you've been responsible with credit for that many years. The account may be worth 30 or 40 points of your payment history. Suppose you have a credit card for 25 years and you close the account. Now let's suppose your next oldest credit card account is only 12 years old. You've just equated yourself with other consumers who've only been responsible with credit for 12 years instead of the 25 years good payment history you actually have.

You don't have to worry about closing out installment accounts. Installment accounts are an important part of your payment history and they will report as closed once you pay them off (car loans, student loans). These types of accounts do not affect you adversely when they are closed. They tend to stay on the credit report indefinitely, which is a good thing if the information is positive.

Raise Your Score by Managing the Amounts Owed

There are three different types of credit, revolving, installment and mortgage credit. Revolving credit is an unsecured line of credit (not backed by any collateral) that you can use up to the available limit. You can pay down the debt and then use it back up to the maximum limit again, as long as you pay the account as agreed. Credit cards are the perfect examples of revolving credit. Revolving accounts remain open as long as the account is in good standing and the consumer chooses to have it open. The amount of credit used is charged an interest rate and there may be other fees involved such as an annual fee or a late payment fee. The amount of the payment due can vary from month to month, but the due date will generally remain the same.

Installment credit has a fixed amount of monthly payments and when those payments are completed the loan is closed (cars, and student loans for example). If you want to take out a new installment loan with the lender after you pay off the old one you typically have to qualify all over again. Mortgage payments, some equity loans, and bank signature loans are installment loans. Installment loans are sometimes backed by collateral such as a house, or boat, but can also be unsecured, such as a student loan, or a personal signature loan from the bank. Paying installment accounts on time as agreed progressively reduces the amount owed and shows responsible credit usage.

Amounts owed on revolving accounts are assessed differently than amounts owed on installment accounts because they are different types of credit. Installment accounts have the most impact on your credit score when you first take them out because they are new accounts. The payment history hasn't been demonstrated yet and the amounts owed are higher. As you make timely payments and gain more equity in the installment (house, car, or student loans paid-off) they look better on your credit report and increase your score. Revolving credit is calculated differently and you can lose as much as 75 points for having maxed out revolving credit accounts.

Credit utilization is the amount of credit you use in relation to the amount of credit you have available to use. 20% of the available credit limit is the ideal percentage to be used on a revolving account. This general rule of thumb means that a credit card with a $1,000 credit limit should never carry a balance over $200. The closer you get to the available credit limit, the lower your score drops. Charging a $1,000 card up to $500 is risky. Maxing out the card to $999 or anything over the $1,000 will cause score to drop drastically, especially if you carry the balance over to the next month. If you use a high percentage of the available credit limit, this is a red flag to a lender. You appear to be overextended and they see you as more of a risk to lend money too. This is why you get declined when you max out the credit limit on an account, and then request an increase with that same lender.

To find the current amount of utilization on a revolving credit card look at your credit report, or the credit card statement. Check the credit limit against the balance to figure out your current utilization. If it's not already at or below 20% figure out a strategy to pay it down. The closer you get to a zero balance the higher your credit score increases. The account doesn't have to be paid off to a zero balance to show an increase in your credit score. As long as the utilization rate is below 20% when your lender reports the account to the CRA you should see an increase in your score.

Most creditors update your account information with the CRA each month. Some creditors report bi-monthly, others report every week. You can ask your lender what date they report your account activity to the CRA. It might be the due date on your credit card statement. Recent 2009 credit card laws require creditors to be consistent with the due dates on consumer credit accounts. The dates can't vary from month-to-month like they used to before the law went into effect. Now that the law is in place, if the bill is due on the 19th of the month, then it should be due on the 19th of every subsequent month. Make sure the balance of that revolving credit account is paid down to 20% of the available limit a few days before the statement due date. Go back and pull your credit score about 3-4 weeks after you paid it to see how it impacted your score.

If you cannot pay all of your revolving credit accounts down to 20% of the available credit limits, I'll give you some pointers on how to get your finances in order later. For now, you might benefit from a strategy called the 80-50-20% strategy. Try getting *all* of your revolving credit accounts down to 80% of the available limits and check your credit score to see the score increase. Once you get the aggregate revolving debt down to 80%, focus on decreasing your total debt down to 50% of the available limits. After you get it all down to 50% work on getting every revolving credit account down to 20%. Paying down your

59

credit card balances is one of the quickest ways to increase your credit score.

Remember the credit score tells a lender/underwriter how likely you are to default on a loan. If you are applying for more credit and already maxed out on your current obligations, you appear desperate for credit. If you're desperate for credit it might be because you're not using your cash responsibly. The last thing a lender wants to do is give you more credit to mismanage.

Some people use one credit card to pay all of their monthly expenses and then pay off the entire balance each month. Suppose you have a credit card with $10,000 limit and you use it to pay $9,999 worth of monthly expenses (mortgage, car-notes, student loans, everything). If your lender reports your credit card activity to the CRA on the 29th of the month you appear to be fully extended at the time of their report. Even if you pay the entire balance down to $0 on the 1st of the following month, at the time your usage was reported to the CRA you were maxed out. If you do that consistently each month, you appear to be regularly over-extended which lowers your credit score.

A better strategy would be to manage your credit utilization and make sure you stay under the $2,000 on that $10,000 credit card. You could also have your credit limit increased to $20,000 or $30,000, if your score and income can support the increase. Another approach would be to spread the utilization across several cards so that you maintain the 20% overall utilization. To protect your score it might be easier to write checks for monthly expenses, use a debit card, or set up an automatic debit your bank account on the due date instead of using a credit card. The idea is to not use a credit card to pay monthly expenses if it causes you to exceed 20% utilization rate.

Raise Your Score By Managing Your Credit History

15% of your credit score is the length of your credit history. The longer you can demonstrate responsible use of credit, the higher your credit scores. If you've had a credit card, or other type of credit account and it has been paid as agreed for 10, 15, or 20 years then it could be worth 30, 40 points or more. This is why people sometimes see their score drop when they close out old, unused accounts. Closing those accounts reduces the length of your credit history, so the credit-scoring model compares you with other consumers who haven't managed credit responsibly for as long as you have.

I once helped a client repair his credit and after his score increased by over 100 points he decided that he had too many credit accounts and closed several without consulting me. He was stunned to find that his score dropped 70 points! You should leave your oldest revolving credit accounts open. Your oldest account being paid as agreed may be worth about 40 points and you could lose those points if you close that account. If there's not a risk of identity theft or other compromises to the account you might want to leave those old accounts open.

It seems simple that you should be able to close credit card accounts that you never use. The problem with closing these accounts is that the credit scoring models reward consumers for having unused credit limits available. When you close unused accounts you eliminate those available credit limits. On the other hand, having cards that are *never* used can cost you points as well. Scoring systems deduct points from consumers with no recent revolving balances reported on their credit. Revolving credit information is less relevant if there are no actual balances on the accounts, and dormant credit cards cost lenders money to maintain your account. FICO can't even generate a score for a consumer without recent activity. The antidote to losing points for dormant cards is to charge just $1 on a card and pay it off before the statement is due. This counts as recent activity and will help increase your score.

Raise Your Score by Managing New Credit

Every time you give a lender your social security number and authorize them to check your credit report, it is a hard inquiry and it decreases your credit score. A hard inquiry tells lenders that you are looking for new credit. Frequent credit inquiries can make you appear as more of a risk depending on several factors. A hard inquiry can take more than 15 points off your credit score depending upon the type of hard inquiry and the time period in which the inquiry was done. I recently worked with a client who lost 19 points through one inquiry for a car loan with her bank. She had been monitoring her reports for several months prior to the loan application and noticed the impact.

A soft inquiry by contrast, doesn't impact your credit score at all. When you check your own credit report, or an employer, government agency, or marketing firm checks your credit report it is always a soft pull and will not impact your score.

Credit reporting agencies (CRAs) exist to sell your information to businesses that have a legitimate interest in consumer's credit histories such as banks and credit card companies. Anytime those lenders review your report and invite you to apply for their cards or services it is always a soft pull because you did not initiate or authorize them to look at your credit report. Even if they don't invite you to apply for the card it is still a soft pull because you didn't initiate the inquiry. Now if you sign on the dotted line and send the "offer" back to the creditor, they will formally review your credit report which *then* becomes a hard inquiry.

The potential lender looks at your credit report during the normal course of business between the lender and the CRA, but you still have to formally "request" credit for it to be a hard inquiry. Your credit report may list these types of soft inquiries in the same column as the inquiries that you authorized through seeking new credit. Know the difference between the two.

If you're shopping for a mortgage, vehicle, or other type of loan you may want to compare rates and terms with different lenders. It is expected that a consumer will comparison shop for the best interest rate on a new house, new car, or a re-finance. As long as the lender is of the same type (all vehicle lenders, or all mortgage brokers) and the hard inquiry occurs within the same 2-week period, multiple hard inquires are typically treated as just one inquiry.

Applying for credit too frequently indicates to a lender that the applicant is desperate to obtain new credit. Limit frequent hard inquiries by relying on cash and managing the credit you already have responsibly. Stop applying for more credit and simply *let your credit rest*. Hard inquiries remain on your credit report for two years, and count against your FICO score for up to a year. Most high credit scorers have about two hard inquiries per year; anything over six inquiries within a year can be viewed as excessive.

Raise Your Score by Managing Credit Types

Lenders like to see consumers use a healthy mix of revolving credit (also called trade lines), installment credit (both secured and unsecured), finance companies, and ideally, mortgage credit. The healthiest mix shows your credit experience with a variety of loan-types. The types of lending institutions you borrow from can also be a factor. Traditional banks and credit unions (Citibank, Chase, Capital One) are viewed as more favorable than certain type of the installment loan companies that target people with challenged credit.

While FICO states that it does not distinguish between types of trade lines, certain types of lenders may not be viewed

63

as favorably as traditional banks and other types of lending institutions. Some finance companies tend to lend primarily to those with challenged credit and charge much higher interest rates for the cost to do business with them. These types of companies dominate the sub-prime market (typically credit scores below 620). Finance company and payday lending accounts may not count for much weight when it comes to increasing your credit score and can actually hurt your score.

Notes/Action Plan

Step 6: Raise Your Credit Score by Creating a Spending Plan to Eliminate Debt

Some of the pointers I mentioned can be immediately applied if there's enough cash flow to pay your bills. If there isn't enough or you're bringing in good money and just can't seem to figure out where it all goes, look at your spending and create a budget. It's important to take a look at what's coming in, and what's going out in order to figure out where to get the money to pay the bills. In order to master paying your bills on time, and keeping your utilization under the suggested 20% ratio, you need to realistically assess your finances. Let's review figuring out the income to debt ratio and some tips on how to get the debt down to a level that works for your budget.

To start, set aside some time to gather all of your bills both paid and unpaid. Open up any spreadsheets, and/or budget plans you may have already created. Organize bills by creditor, amounts owed, and/or due date. Categorize things in an order that makes sense to you so that you'll be more likely to implement the strategies. Open any bills that might have been sitting around unopened and figure out how you're going to sort and group them. Sample categories might be "pay now, pay later, pending, file". Identify the total amount due on each bill or credit account. Determine what the interest rates are, if any, and the amount of the monthly payments. ***Know how much you owe.***

Now that you've figured out what you owe, compute your consumer debt-to-disposable income ratio. There are different types of ratios that lenders use to assess your creditworthiness. This particular ratio helps you figure out your consumer debt load.

Your debt payments-to-disposable income ratio is the percentage of your monthly income (net) that goes towards

66

paying your monthly debts (excluding your mortgage or rent). Lenders look at this number when deciding if they want to lend you money and at what rate. It's as important as the credit score and worth figuring out. Disposable income is the money left over after federal, state, and local taxes have been deducted from your paycheck. Money left over after all the living expenses are paid is discretionary income. Calculate this ratio by adding up all of the debt you owe (minus mortgage or rent) and divide your monthly disposable income by the amount of debt you owe:

Debt owed (exclude mortgage)/monthly income (after taxes/net pay) = ratio
ex: $1500(debt)/$5000(monthly income) = .30 or 30% D-T-I ratio.

Add up all your debt (exclude mortgage/rent): _____
Divide it by your monthly income (net): _____
Your D-T-I Ratio is: _____

If your debt payment- to -disposable income ratio is:

- Less than 15% - things are under pretty much under control
- 15-20% - use caution when taking on additional debt if at all
- 21% or higher – get help from a financial counselor or professional

In order to figure out where you're going financially, it's important to assess where you are now. A budget/spending plan is a highly personal and dynamic tool. It changes as your circumstances changes and cannot be dictated by anyone else's standards but your own. What works for your budget might not work for a friend or family member's budget and vice-versa. Think of your spending plan or budget as a blueprint, a way to control your spending patterns and direct your income to buy the things that you really need, and some of the things you really want.   A comprehensive budget/spending plan includes a net worth statement, a listing of all the monthly income coming in, and all the monthly expenses going out. You can also include an action plan to reach the financial goals you set for yourself.

Start with the end in mind.   Just as we assessed motivation for improving the credit score, what's the motivation for creating a spending plan? Financial values form the basis of your spending plan and determine how you define goals, and monetize the cost of each goal. Motivation *and* inspiration are needed to accomplish your goal.   It takes time to reach a goal and you have to be able to stay on track. Financial goals are defined by the number of months or years it takes to reach a particular goal.

Short-term goals (can be completed in 1-2 years)

Goal	Cost	#Months to Deadline	Savings Per Month

Mid-term goals (can be completed in 3-5 years)

Goal	Cost	#Months to Deadline	Savings Per Month

Long-term goals (longer than 5 years)

Goal	Cost	#Months to Deadline	Savings Per Month

A well known acronym in reaching goals is make sure that they are S.M.A.R.T. goals:

S – Specific

M - Measureable

A - Attainable

R - Realistic

T – Time bound

An example of a short-term SMART goal would be to increase your credit score by 100 points in less than 12 months. How you reach that goal specifically will depend upon the actions you take to create improvement. Paying down the balance due on 3 credit cards in 9 months by 30%, which puts you under the recommended 20% utilization rate, might be one way of reaching this SMART goal.

Another goal might involve increasing your savings. Setting aside $100 per month in an interest earning account starting in January gives you at least $1,200 by December. It's going to feel a lot nicer walking into the toy store with cash to spend as opposed to whipping out the credit cards, hoping none of them get declined at check-out. Determine your goals and set a deadline for yourself. Divide the costs by the number of months it would take to reach the goal. Factor this amount into your monthly savings to ensure that you set aside enough money to meet the goal. Savings should be a line item when you list expenses on your spending plan.

The net-worth statement is useful in determining where you stand as of today, and can be useful to measure financial progress as time goes on. It is a statement that tallies what you own, minus what you owe. Think of it as a financial snapshot or Instagram, showing the picture of where you are at this moment in your financial life. The number you produce is dynamic and will change according to the decisions that you make from this moment on.

Net Worth Worksheet

Assets	Value	Liabilities	Value
Cash on hand	$	Mortgage balance due	$
Checking Accounts	$	Auto balance due	$
Saving Accounts	$	Bank loan balance due	$
Bonds	$	Student loans	$
Certificates of Deposit (CDs)	$	Credit card balance(s) due	$
Stocks	$	Personal loans	$
Mutual Funds	$	Taxes due	$
Cash value of life insurance policy	$		
Home (Market Value)	$		
Rental property	$		
Vehicles	$		
Home Furnishings	$		
Total	$	Total	$

Total Assets	Minus	Total Liabilities equals	Net Worth

In the first column of your net worth statement, list all of the assets that you own and their dollar value. List all of the money you have in your pocket, in your checking and savings accounts, and in certificates-of-deposit (CDs). List the value of any stock, bonds, mutual funds, 401K, Individual Retirement Accounts (IRA), Thrift Savings Program (TSP) and the cash value of any whole life insurance policies that you may own. Be careful not to include the value of any term life insurance policies here (they build no cash value). List the amount your home(s) would sell for if you were to put it on the market today, and the resale value of any vehicles you own (Kelly blue book, NADA). Include your cars, motorcycles, boats, ATVs or any other motorized vehicles.

Also list items such as furniture, art, and any collections that you may own, things you could sell today if you had too. While it is obviously harder to liquidate furniture, if you had to do an estate sale, or sell things on eBay or craigslist, how much could you expect to get for these items? Look for the high dollar items (worth over $500) such as HDTV's, gaming computers, high-end electronics, jewelry, and designer purses. Estimate the value of any coin, sword, gun, comic book, doll collections, or any works of art, and family heirlooms with high dollar value. These are all assets that can be sold for money, if necessary. Add up the total value in the asset column of your net worth statement.

Next, tally all of the liabilities you're responsible for. Here is where you'd list the amounts owed on any personal loans, credit cards, and student loans. Also include the payoff amounts of any of the vehicles you listed as assets and the pay-off balance of any mortgages. Add up all the liabilities that you owe. Subtract the total amount of your liabilities from the total amount of your assets; this number is your net worth.

It can be a negative number or a positive number. It is only a starting point and you get to determine how high or low that number moves from here on out. Increasing this number can even become a new financial goal. As you decrease what you owe, and increase owning more valuable assets you will increase

73

your net-worth. You should evaluate your net worth periodically. There are budget tools online that will automatically calculate your net worth for you and update you on a weekly, or monthly basis. Track it consistently to assess your financial position and determine your financial progress.

The next part of the spending plan will include listing all of the money coming into your household. List the total amount of monthly income for yourself, your spouse, or anyone else who contributes to your household. Include all employment and pensions. Note compensation received for hobbies, and businesses you work on the side. Include any social security, retirement pay, disability pay, child support, alimony, gift inheritances, insurance payouts, or any public assistance monies that you may receive. Be sure to deduct for the taxes you pay and contributions to your 401K, IRA, and 529 type plans. Add up all of the money available each month for you to use to pay your monthly expenses, fund your savings and investment accounts, pay down credit card debt, and spend at your discretion

Income	Estimated Amount
Wages, salary, tips	
Income from Dividends	
Investment Income	
Social Security Income	
Retirement/Pension	
Child Support	
Alimony	
Unemployment	
Disability	
Government Payments	
Winnings	
Scholarship, Fellowships, Grants	
Spouses Income	
Inheritances/Gifts	
Rental Income	
Total:	

Deductions	Estimated Amount
Federal Taxes	
FICA (Social Security)	
FICA (Medicare)	
State Income Tax	
Medical	
Dental	
Life Insurance	
401K	
Total:	

Now let's itemize all of the expenses going out of the household each month. If you're not already doing so, get in the habit of paying yourself first. Note expenditures going into your short, mid, and long term savings accounts. If something comes out of your paycheck automatically and you've already annotated it in the income section you shouldn't repeat it here under expenses (like 401K deductions).

Fixed expenses are items like your mortgage/rent, and car insurance. These items are typically a fixed amount and do not fluctuate from month to month. Next list all of your variable expenses and pay close attention because this is where we typically find hidden cash in the budget to pay off debt. Include categories such as electricity, gas, water, cable, Internet, cell phones, gas, groceries, lunch money for you and your children. List the amount of money spent each month on haircuts, clothing, dining-out, birthday gifts, hobbies, wine, cigarettes, entertainment, transportation etc. If there are any expenses that are paid annually, or quarterly, such as your vehicle registration(s), calculate the annual amount of those fees and divide by 12 to find the monthly amount to add to the budget.

Expense	Estimated Amount
Rent/Mortgage	
Maintenance/Repairs	
Insurance	
Car payment	
Child support payment	
Child care/elder care	
Credit card payment	
Groceries	
Electricity/Gas/Water	
Personal Hygiene	
Private Lessons	
Cable/Internet	
House telephone	
Cell phones	
Transportation	
Medical/Dental Expenses	
Pet Care	
Entertainment/Hobbies	
Clothing	
Total:	

Subtract your monthly expenses from your monthly income. If you have more income than expenses, than you have a surplus. Review strategies to apply that surplus towards eliminating debt while building up your emergency reserve fund. Most financial experts recommend that you save at least 3-6 months living expenses in your reserve fund. If the monthly expenses are about $3,000 then shoot for $9,000 - $18,000 in reserve. Start where you are with your emergency fund. If you can save at least $1,000 dedicated to your emergency reserve fund, you can use that money to offset unexpected financial expenses as they occur.

Summary of Income, Savings, Living Expenses

Total Combined Net Income	
Savings & Investments	-
Living Expenses	-
Amount Left to Pay Debt	=
Total Monthly Debt Payment	-
Surplus or Deficit	
Debt to Income Ratio	

Your emergency reserve money needs to easily accessible so put it into a Money Market Deposit Account (MMDA), or some CD's that you can liquidate quickly if necessary. Ladder your CDs so they mature on a monthly basis, always easily accessible to you without incurring any penalties. It is recommended that you keep your emergency reserve money in cash bank products to avoid risk. The Federal Deposit Insurance Corporation (FDIC) insures each bank account for up to $250,000 should something happen to the bank. The NCUA insures the money you have on deposit with most credit unions for the same amount.

79

If you have more expenses than income then you have a deficit. You will have to use strategies to decrease expenses, and increase income in order to find more money to pay down debt and bulk up your savings. There are several ways to solve a deficit. I'm going to spend the rest of this chapter giving you specific strategies to control spending and have more money available to pay down debt.

Almost everyone can benefit from taking a long, hard look at exactly where the money is going, doesn't matter if you have a surplus or a deficit. A 30-day tracking sheet allows you to do just that. Write down every dollar you spend on everything for 30 days to figure out where the money goes. You may not even need to track for the entire 30 days. Sometimes we can see where the bulk of our money goes after tracking for just 7-14 days. We tell ourselves we want our money to do *one thing* (ex: use our money to pay down debt) but what we actually *do* with our money is often an entirely different thing (like spend it all on dining out, good wine and entertainment). The tracking sheet tells the truth about what we choose to do with our money. Sometimes coming face-to-face with that truth is all that's necessary to make real and lasting changes.

Some people prefer to save receipts as a method of tracking their spending, but not every purchase can be verified with a paper receipt. If you spend money at Starbucks, or McDonalds, the supermarket, on eBay or craigslist, you should write it down on the tracking sheet. If you loan someone $5 bucks, contribute $20 towards someone's gas, or put $10 in the office kitty to celebrate a co-workers birthday, you should write it down. If you eat out and use your credit card for the meal, but leave the tip in cash, you should track both actions on your sheet.

Your spouse should do his or her own tracking sheet if he or she is also responsible for the spending. The two of you can compare your lists daily, weekly or at the end of the month. Keep in mind, a budget is dynamic and highly personal, so it's not about right or wrong when it comes to the tracking the spending. It's about accurately assessing where your cash is going and *then* figuring out what works for your budget or spending plan. After reviewing where your cash is going you might want to reassess your spending and plan new ways to redirect where you want the money to go.

Daily Expense Tracking Sheet

Date	Item & Category	Amount

A helpful tool to use in assessing your purchases is to begin separating "wants" vs. "needs". Most expenses can be placed into either category. In my house, cable is a "want". We've figured out that we don't spend much time at home watching TV and we're not attached to any particular shows, so we got rid of cable TV. We get about 100 free channels using a HDTV, which *is* an antenna and maximizes the free programming we find in the air (go to http://antennaweb.org/ for more information). While cable is a "want" in our house, it could be a "need" for a stay-at- home mom with three young kids under the age of five. Cable TV with the Disney channel, and Nick Jr. might be a *lifeline* for her. A financial professional once said, "If you can use it, eat it, or wear it, it's not a need". Ask yourself "do I really *need* to get the latest model car, or do I really *need* to eliminate some of this debt"?

One of the best ways to improve your credit score is to master the management of your cash so that you are never relying on your credit cards. Using credit cards can lull you into a false sense of security, thinking you have more money than you really do. In order to pay down the debt and increase the credit score you will have to limit your use of credit cards.

When I see a client with 8 or more credit cards in their wallet and the credit report shows that the client is burdened with debt, I recommend getting those cards out of the wallet and "freezing" them.... I mean *literally* putting the credit cards on ice. Drop the credit cards in a bowl or cup of water and put them in the freezer. More drastic measures may involve burning the cards, or cutting them up. Do whatever you have to do to get the cards out of your wallet or purse. Put them away in a safety deposit box until you can get control of the spending. I suggest you *don't* close out the credit card account (unless you want to see your credit score plummet) but you do have to put some distance between you and the plastic.

In order to master your cash you have to become re-acquainted with it. Studies have shown that poor spending habits and using credit cards is the number one reason most people get into debt. Using credit cards can be addictive, we pull out the plastic and we spend, and spend, and spend. We do this because we are not attached to the plastic the way we are attached to our cash. That's why they give you chips to play with at the gambling casinos. You play the games all night long and when the debt gets called in at the end of the night, you're surprised to find out how much you really owe! It's easy to play with chips; you're not attached to the plastic.

To illustrate this point think of that one thing you *love* to buy when you walk into the mall. Maybe it's shoes, or video games, or make-up, or something from the electronics store. Now let's suppose that item is on sale for $99 and you have $100 cash in your pocket, and a credit card with at least $100 available on it. What are you going to use to pay for that item? Are you going to use the cash or the credit card? Most folks will use the credit card because it's so much easier to whip out that card, than to part with the money. It's a lot harder to spend the cash, because you're more attached to it.... You work so hard for the money.

In order to break the spending cycle and get you reacquainted with your cash, you have to get the cards out of your wallet to make them less accessible. You may get a little desperate and decide you need to go home and get your credit cards to buy something you saw on sale earlier that day. The time that it would take to thaw out the frozen cards would be enough time for you to really think about whether or not this item is a want or a need.

One of the strongest methods to control spending is to use the envelope system on a strictly cash basis. Fixed expenses can be paid automatically from your checking account as they are due, but some variable expenses need to go on the envelope system. For example, let's use a variable expense group like groceries and we'll include food, toilet paper, toothpaste, deodorant, and cat food in that category. Let's say that you typically spend about $600 per month on groceries. Take four different envelopes and put $150 cash in each envelope. Now, assuming the perfect month has four weeks, and that the perfect week begins on a Sunday, start spending out of the first envelope week #1.

Every time you go to the grocery store you take cash out of the envelope to pay for your purchases that first week. When there is no more cash in that envelope, it doesn't matter what day of the week it is, spending for groceries for that week is *done*! Seriously.... even if there's more than enough money in your savings, or on a credit card, you *cannot* spend any more money on groceries until the next Sunday. If it's Thursday night and there's no more money in that envelope then it's time to get creative. Eat the food you have stored in the cabinets, raid your pantry to fix fun meals, get creative with the ramen, or get yourself invited out to eat. You do whatever you have to do to make it to the next week, but don't dare touch another envelope until Sunday.

Following this method (especially when you have more than enough) will give you the discipline to put the brakes on impulse spending when you're in the store. The envelope system is the strongest method to control spending. Suddenly those impulse items at the cash register aren't so compelling anymore. You may even find yourself sticking to your shopping list and using other shopping tricks to stay on budget. At the end of the month re-evaluate your "groceries" category and allocate more or less money to that category for the next month if necessary. Use the envelope system with other variable items like dining out, and hobbies. Activities like golfing, shopping for clothes, video gaming, and crafting can all be put on the envelope system.

Some people think they are better off putting an allotted amount on a store debit card and using that exclusively. This might work for some but I find it best to use cash when you're trying to control spending. I have friends who use a debit card when shopping in Wal-Mart. They buy a $200 store card every month on the first and use it exclusively for Wal-Mart. When that $200 is gone they don't go to Wal-Mart again until the following month. While this works for my friends, it might not work for others because the debit card is still plastic and you need to conquer the plastic-habit in order to control spending. Most people go into a store like Wal-Mart intending to buy a gallon of milk, but they come out with throw pillows, mirrors and a lawn mower. Using cash when shopping will rein in the impulse spending and cause you to evaluate if you really need the electric-fondue maker when all you really had on your shopping list was orange-juice and diapers?

Do this for each variable expense and re-evaluate the category monthly. Take a hard look at how you can trim, cut, and slash those categories. This is the area where you're going to find the money you didn't think you had to get out of credit card debt. Review your list of variable expenses to see which items can be comfortably eliminated (temporarily or permanently) and which items can be reduced. Can you ditch the cable TV; reduce the cell phone bill or internet plan? How about suspending home phone service and using cell phones and alternatives like the Magic Jack?

Review the extra add-ons you pay with your bills every month. Do you really need credit card insurance, if you're covered by your employer's unemployment insurance, disability insurance, and/or life insurance? Do you need this extra protection on credit cards when you don't carry a balance or you're working a plan to get out of debt and build your emergency reserve? Can you suspend some of the monthly subscriptions that you don't even use like the wine and coffee club, the gym, the credit score monitoring company, monthly massage account, or garden club that sends automatic offerings? These monthly subscriptions can automatically take money out of your checking account so you don't even notice the $250 a year that could be going toward debt elimination instead.

There are many sample budget templates available on-line and most of them are free. You can print them out and fill them in with a pencil each month, or you can manage your budget with a spreadsheet, using programs like Excel or

85

https://www.mint.com/. These sites use bank-level encryption and allow you to enter and manage all of your checking, savings, investment, assets, and credit accounts in one place. You can build a budget and the program will monitor your progress and send you updates as they occur. There are smart-phone applications that you can download that will track the progress of any pay-down strategy you implement. Your bank might provide a program that allows you to manage your personal finances online and through your cell-phone.

There are generally acceptable percentages you can use as a guideline when determining how much money to allocate for various categories in your budget. While you might spend more or less of your monthly income on the following categories, these suggested percentages are offered to help you achieve financial freedom sooner:

- Housing : no more than 30% of your monthly income
- Food: 15-30%
- Utilities : 4-7%
- Transportation: 6-20%
- Installment loans: less than 20%
- Savings : at least 10%

Housing, student loans, and car insurance are fixed expenses. The name "fixed" implies that these amounts are non-negotiable, however to balance a budget deficit you may have to re-adjust these "fixed" amounts. There are some things you can do to lower these expenses.

Choosing a higher deductible on your car insurance may lower your insurance payments without lowering the amount of coverage. If you currently have a $250 deductible on your car insurance policy, consider raising that deductible to $1,000 especially if you already have the $1,000 sitting in your emergency fund earning interest. By raising the deductible you can lower the cost of the policy premium by as much as 40%. If you don't have that money in tucked away in savings and you're prone to accidents don't gamble with the insurance policy by raising the deductible. Should something happen you will have to pay the $1,000 before your insurance company will pay, so only use this strategy if you have adequate savings.

To save money on housing, consider moving to a less expensive apartment if you're a renter, or consider refinancing your home to lower monthly mortgage payments. Sharing space with a roommate is also an option to lower your monthly expenses. Always crunch the numbers and compare the costs of each decision to see which one would be the most advantageous.

To eliminate debt you have decrease expenses. While credit card companies love customers who carry balances and pay high interest rates their primary concern is that you pay back the money you borrow. Call your lenders directly and let them know about your efforts to eliminate debt, ask if there are any programs available to help. You can let them know you are experiencing a temporary hardship, and ask for lower interest rates, waive the annual fees, reverse late charges, and over-the-limit-fees. If you have a good credit score and other credit card companies are vying for your business, call your creditors and let them know you are considering moving the accounts to other creditors. Ask if they can offer more competitive interest rates than what you currently pay.

Creditors are highly motivated to negotiate with you.... they want you to pay back the money you owe. See if they will offer you the privilege of skipping a few payments. This might allow time to apply extra payments to other accounts, or meet the minimum payment on other items. Interest will continue to accrue if your lender allows you to skip a few payments. Still, it's better to have your lenders approval to miss payments than to just skip making them on your own. This could cost extra money in late fees, and cause your credit score to plunge. Call your creditors and work with them to come up with an acceptable payment plan.

Your Name
Your Address
City, State, Zip Code

Date

Creditor's Address
City, State, Zip

Re: Account #

Dear Sir or Madam:

I am writing to request a temporary change in my repayment terms of my account with you. I'm going through a financial crisis and may not be to continue the current payment plan. I find it absolutely necessary to ask for an alterative payment plan from each of my creditors until my financial situation improves.

I do not plan to file for bankruptcy and I do not intend to default on this debt. I have completely reviewed my budget and find it necessary that I ask your assistance in determining the best way to repay you under the circumstances.

I am asking that you accept a monthly payment of $_____ instead of my regularly scheduled payment of $_____ that I've been making on time for the past few months (years).

I can resume making the regularly scheduled payments as soon as the financial crisis is resolved. I hope you will seriously consider my request and I would be grateful if you honored it. I thank you in advance for your consideration in this matter.

Sincerely,

Your Name

When cutting expenses in your budget, make sure the cuts are both necessary and practical. Riding a bike to work may save you money on gas but is it practical for your lifestyle? If riding the bike home causes you to arrive later to your child's day care center to pick him up and you're assessed late fees, are you truly saving money? How do you get the baby home on the bike anyway? Is that expense/risk worth it? Pushing an electric lawn mower may save you money over the gas-powered mower, but if it costs you an entire Saturday afternoon to complete the job, is it the best use of your time? Time is money, so figure out the best use of both to meet your budget goals.

Figure out how you can increase income. The more money you have coming in, the more money you'll have available to pay down debt and build up savings. If your spouse or live-in partner doesn't work, the obvious answer would seem to get a job, but make sure you crunch the numbers first. If your spouse has to spend extra money on childcare, gas, wardrobe, taxes, and food does that truly offset any money they might earn? Are there other alternatives? Would it be better for the stay-at-home partner to explore starting a home-based business? Does that spouse have a skill-set that would support free-lancing? Can they blog, cater, use hobbies and skills to make money? Are there any telecommuting opportunities that your spouse could apply for?

A resource I've recommended over the years is The Rat Race Rebellion. This is a website many military spouses use to find legitimate work-at-home opportunities. No envelope stuffing here. You'll find customer service positions for national companies (Amazon, 1-800-Contacts, 1-800-Pro-Flowers). The Rat Race Rebellion connects you with employers offering telecommuting, free-lance, or work-at-home positions earning $15 per hour or more, depending upon the position. Go to http://www.ratracerebellion.com/ for more information. Check the record of any complaints a company may have at: http://www.bbb.org, before you decide to do business with them.

When looking for money to pay off debts, why not check and see if anyone owes you money? Inheritances, unclaimed bank funds, utility deposits and other monies usually end up in your state's escheat office. People that owe you money may not search for you as relentlessly as the people you owe money too. The National Association of Unclaimed Property Administrators has a website with links that allow you to look up every state you ever lived in to see if you anyone owes you money. Select your state and type in the your name. Include maiden names, or other forms of the name you might have used when you lived in that state. You might find a few investment firms, insurance companies, utility companies, and state tax offices that have funds owed to you. To find unclaimed money in your state go to: http://www.unclaimed.org/. The state of Colorado owed me a couple of dollars for overpaying my taxes a few years ago. I found out when I typed my name in the search engine of the following website and discovered I had a claim:

http://www.missingmoney.com/

To find federal or government funds that may be due you go to: http://www.usa.gov/Citizen/Topics/Government-Unclaimed-Money.shtml

You may be able to find cash to repay debt and build savings by going shopping in your own home. Edit your possessions to determine what is underutilized and could possibly have re-sale value. High-end purses, clothing, and furniture can all be resold, or consigned. Some of these barely used purchases were charged on credit cards still accruing interest. Is this the best use of your money? You probably won't recoup what you paid for the item but the money it could bring in a sale may offset the cost of storing and maintaining a barely used item.

Reduce clutter and sell some things you have lying around the house. Be ruthless in editing those storage rooms too. If you paid $40 per month for a 5x10 storage room over the past few years, that's $480 a year you're spending to store stuff that you may never use. That money could possibly be spent on something else. Are you storing furniture, appliances and electronics that will be outdated by the time you get it out of storage? If so sell the contents of the storage room and eliminate that bill. Use the proceeds towards debt elimination. If you donate unused items don't forget to get a receipt for tax purposes.

Once you've figured out how to increase income and reduce expenses review strategies to repay debt and build your reserves. Power-pay and debt snowball are methods used to reduce debt quickly. Pick the card with the highest interest rate, or lowest balance due and pay that card off first before rolling that payment over to the next card. This forms a snowball of larger payments that build and build until the debt is eliminated.

Debt Snowball Chart

Credit Card	Total Payoff	Minimum Due	Snowball Payment
Visa	$1,000	$50	$50 +$100 = $150
MasterCard	$2,000	$50	$200
Discover	$3,000	$50	$250

In this example you have 3 credit cards with balances due of $3,000, 2,000, and $1,000 each. You're currently making the minimum payments of $50 per month on each card, but you don't see any real progress towards eliminating the debt. Assuming the interest rates were all equal (9%) you could continue to make the minimum payments on the $3,000 and $2,000 cards, ($50) and add an extra $100 per month towards the $1,000 Visa card so that you're now paying $150 per month on that card. At 9% interest rate it would take about 22 months to have that $1,000 card paid off if you continue to make just the minimum payment. Paying $150 per month gets the card paid off in just 7 months. This example assumes you're not making new charges on the credit card as you are paying it down.

Once you have the $1,000 card paid off, take that $150 and add it to the next card you were paying $50 a month on. By paying $200 per month on the $2,000 MasterCard, you'll have that card paid off in 11 months. When that card is paid off you can add the $200 payment to the $50 you were already paying on the $3,000 Discover card. With $250 per month, it'll take you 13 months to be debt free. This is how to get the debt eliminated.

Go to http://www.bankrate.com/calculators/credit-cards/credit-card-payoff-calculator.aspx for excellent calculators to pay down debt. Go to https://powerpay.org to create a plan to pay down debt. I can't stress enough in order to see real improvement of your credit score, get the credit utilization down to 20% on all of your revolving accounts. Getting the balances further reduced to zero will greatly impact your personal finances. You need to use credit cards to generate a credit score, but limit your use to one or two cards. You can make minor purchases (gas, candy) and pay the bill each month, rotating the credit cards if you have more than one.

Debt consolidation and Debt Management Plans are options when the debt load becomes impossible. Consolidation loans are given at banks, credit unions, or other financial institutions and are based on your credit score. You take out a loan for the total amount of debt you owe and use the proceeds to pay off each debt, combining several accounts into one manageable payment. To qualify for a large consolidation loan ($25,000 or more) you'll need a high credit score, substantial income and/or collateral to secure the loan.

One way to qualify for a consolidation loan is get a second mortgage on your property, or a home-equity-line-of-credit. This choice could jeopardize your home if you don't cut up the credit cards you pay off. Seriously question taking unsecured credit card and student loan debt, and turning it into secured debt, backed by the security of your home. If you default on the consolidation loan you could lose the house. Until you start making regular payments on time as agreed with the new consolidation loan you credit score will go down a bit when you take out a consolidation loan.

A Debt Management Plan (DMP) may be an alternative for insurmountable debt. A certified credit counselor at a reputable debt management agency will review your current budget and debt load during your initial appointment. You'll receive an estimate of how much the principal and/or interest rate can be reduced on each account, and if the late fees can be waived. The agency negotiates with your creditors on your behalf and combines all of your accounts into one monthly payment. The agency charges a small monthly fee of about $20 for the service. Most credit counseling agencies that offer DMPs have successfully negotiated plans with various creditors before. These agencies are non-profit and receive funding from businesses they've built a reciprocal relationship with. Banks, credit cards companies and other types of lenders support the DMP, because it's a chance to be repaid some of the money consumers owe them.

Meet face-to-face with a Financial Counselor for a confidential financial session. During your first meeting you'll review all of your debt obligations to determine if you have enough income to support a debt management plan. If you were formerly paying $1,200 per month in credit card, private student loans, and medical debt the agency could possibly get it all reduced to about $500 per month with a $20 monthly fee for the next 3 years. You'll have to agree not to apply for any new credit or use credit cards while on the DMP.

It's important that you make on-time payments to the agency so they can disperse the funds to your creditors in a timely manner. As you successfully make the payments on the DMP, many creditors will re-age the accounts, eliminating the effect of late payments you've made in the past. New payments are updated on your credit report as long as you stick to the plan. If you miss payments your agency can drop you from the DMP and the creditors will resume contacting you directly for their money. If you successfully complete the plan your credit score should be higher than it was when you began. Some creditors will re-activate your accounts with them and increase your credit limits now that you've demonstrated responsible credit card management.

Be wary of credit counselors that seem to push debt management plans without reviewing your individual circumstances, or offering any other alternatives to improve your budget/credit score. Check to see if the agency gets any sort of benefit or commission by signing you up for a DMP. If they recommend a DMP without knowing the specifics of your situation, they may not be acting in your best interest. Find another credit counselor.

Find a credit counselor through the following links:

- U.S. bankruptcy court maintains a list of approved credit counseling agencies at:

  http://www.justice.gov/ust/eo/bapcpa/ccde/cc_approved.htm

- US Dept. of Housing and Urban Development has a list of certified housing counselors that can help with mortgage related credit challenges at:
  http://www.hud.gov/offices/hsg/sfh/hcc/hcs.cfm

- The National Foundation of Credit Counseling has a list of member agencies at: http://www.nfcc.org

- The Association for Financial Counseling - Planning – Education (AFCPE) has a listing of Accredited Financial Counselors and Certified Housing Counselors. To find a certified professional visit the AFCPE website at: http://members.afcpe.org/search

Check to see if any complaints have been filed against a credit counseling agency at the Better Business Bureau: http://www.bbb.org/

File a complaint against any debt-relief service companies with The Consumer Finance Protection Bureau: http://www.consumerfinance.gov/

It's wise to assemble a team of financial professionals to help you stay on track with your financial goals. You might include an Enrolled Agent, to help maximize your tax benefits, and a Financial Advisor to help with investment, and insurance decisions. An Accredited Financial Counselor (AFC®) will review your budget, come up with debt elimination strategies, and help maximize your credit score management. AFCs will also educate you on various investments, but they typically do not sell securities or insurance products, nor do they take over the management of your portfolio. Financial Counselors help with everyday life decisions like refinancing your house, buying a vehicle, and managing student loans. Some are well-versed tax professionals, and others have extensive information on estate planning to help you maximize your relationship with your law or tax professional. Some Financial Counselors are also Certified Financial Planners (CFP) and may offer investment advice.

A Financial Counselor can position you to gain wealth, but you don't have to earn a six-figure income to use one. Some multi-million dollar lottery winners, and highly paid sports figures wish they had consulted with a Financial Counselor before they starting managing their wealth. Many former millionaires aren't as prosperous because they trusted their assets to "financial advisors" who did not have their best interests at heart and lost money in bad investments. Working with a Financial Counselor to increase your level of personal financial education can help you ask better questions of your

Financial Advisors. If you're just starting out in your career, in college, or changing life circumstances, a Financial Counselor can help you determine a plan to meet day to day living expenses and set some goals for the future. A Financial Counselor in private practice might charge an hourly fee. Many colleges, military installations, and community service agencies have counselors available for free. Check potential counselors and/or agencies out with the Better Business Bureau.

Notes/Action Plan

Step 7: Raise Your Credit Score Through Credit Repair/Debt Negotiation

The Internet, radio, and television ads are cluttered with companies that promise to fix your credit report and help you get a higher credit score. Some of them even promise to get any type of negative information removed from your credit report. You should be suspicious of anyone who tries to offer you a quick fix. These con-artists use shady methods that are sometimes illegal. A credit repair scam can cost thousands of dollars, providing no debt relief. In some cases you could be subject to criminal charges. There is nothing a credit repair company can legally do for you that you can't do for yourself. If they don't tell you this, you're probably dealing with a sham credit repair company.

You have the right to sue a credit repair agency that violates the Credit Repair Organization Act. This law was designed to prohibit deceptive practices, but catching up with these questionable firms to hold them accountable may be next to impossible. Signs that you might be dealing with a credit repair sham include:

- Being asked to pay up-front for credit repair services. By law credit repair firms aren't supposed to charge you until they finish the job.

- If they suggest you obtain a "new" social security number, or use an E.I.N. number instead of your social security #to apply for new credit. This is illegal and could land you in jail.

- If they tell you NOT to contact your creditors directly and prevent you from updating your accounts. A reliable agency wouldn't prohibit you from following-up on their activities.

As a consumer you have a right to dispute negative inaccurate information directly with the credit reporting agency (CRA), and to have that information verified, deleted or updated. You are entitled to have most adverse information removed after 7 years, but there may be some instances when you'd like to settle an overdue account on your credit report from 4 or 5 years ago. Maybe you're trying to qualify for a home loan, or pass a background check and you can't afford to wait the full 7 years for the item to come off of your credit report. It might be to your advantage to settle the matter now.

To be perfectly clear, *you do not have a right* to have accurate negative information removed from your credit report. If a creditor is willing to settle the debt and remove the negative entry it would *totally be as a courtesy to you.* The negotiation must be done directly with the creditor, not the CRA. Getting the account settled and removed may increase your credit score. It could help you qualify for offers you wouldn't normally receive with an outstanding negative account on your credit report.

The creditor may be willing to settle with you for less than the full amount. If the original creditor has charged-off the bad debt it might have been sold to a collection agency. Third party collection agencies pay pennies on the dollar to buy debt from the original creditor so there may be room for negotiation and leverage to get the information removed from your credit report. For example, you might have owed the original creditor $1,000 on the account and the debt was sold to a collection agency for $100. The debt collector might be willing to settle for less than the $1,000 in exchange for removal of the negative information from your credit report. An account that went to collections can decrease your score by 50 points or more. One of my clients had a collection account for $52 in medical collections settled and removed. He showed me his updated credit score several weeks later. The score increased by 50 points at one CRA. Getting collection accounts paid and/or removed from your credit report can increase your score tremendously.

99

The Fair Debt Collection Practices Act (FDCPA) is a federal law that prohibits debt collectors from using abusive, unfair, or deceptive practices to collect from you. This law regulates the behavior of collection agencies, the lawyers who collect debts on a regular basis and the people who buy delinquent debt in order to collect on it. The FDCPA covers all personal debt that an individual or family may incur, including credit card, auto loan, medical bill, and mortgage credit.

Debt collectors cannot threaten you with violence, use obscene or profane language, or repeatedly use the phone to harass, abuse, or otherwise annoy you. A debt collector can't call you before 8 a.m. or after 9p.m. and may not contact you at work if they are told you are not allowed to receive calls there. A debt collector can only contact a third party about you once, to find out your address, your phone number, and where you work. They cannot discuss your debt with any third parties. Debt collectors are only permitted to discuss your debt with you, your spouse, or your attorney. If you advise a debt collector that an attorney represents you the debt collector must contact that attorney directly.

If a debt collector is abusive you can sever all communication with him/her. You have the right to issue a "cease and desist" letter. Send the letter by certified mail, with return receipt requested so that you'll have a record of when the collection agency signed for and received your letter. Keep a copy of the letter in your records. Once the collection agency receives this notice they can only contact you once more to say they're taking a specific action against you. They can only say they're taking specific action against you (like suing you) if they're actually going to do it. It's illegal for them to threaten a lawsuit against you if they don't intend to follow-through with it.

If you send a debt collector a written notice saying that you don't think you owe the money, or request verification of the debt, the collector must stop contacting you until they can send you written verification of the debt (like a copy of the bill).

Your Name
Your Address
City, State, Zip Code

Date

Creditor/Collection Agency Address
City, State, Zip

Re: Account #

Dear Sir or Madam:

This is to inform you that I recently checked my credit report and noticed a collection account from your agency. I have never been notified of this collection and this is the first time I'm hearing about it. I am not refusing to pay, but I am requesting that you provide me with evidence that I have a legal obligation to pay you.

The Fair Debt Collection Practices Act states that I have the right to request a validation of this debt. I am aware that until you validate this debt, your agency can neither continue collection activities against me, nor report this information as accurate on my credit report. It is my hope that you will avoid any non-compliance action that would put your agency at risk of violating Federal Trade Commission (FTC) and The State Attorney General's Office mandates.

Please provide me with any agreement that authorizes you to collect on this alleged debt, along with any agreement that bears signature of the alleged debtor promising to pay the creditor.

Sincerely,

Your Name

To see other provisions of the Fair Debt Collection Practices Act go to: www.consumer.ftc.gov/articles. If you have a problem with debt collectors violating the law you can report them to your state Attorney General's office at: http://www.naag.org/. You can also contact the Federal Trade Commission at:

http://www.ftc.gov/os/statutes/fdcpajump.shtm.

Find out what type of collection agency is contacting you. Some collection agencies are divisions within the original creditor's organization. Others are third party debt collectors who buy debt from original creditors. These collection agencies make money by collecting the entire amount of the debt owed from the consumer. Some collection agencies get paid a percentage of the amount collected from the consumer. They try to collect the entire outstanding balance so that they can get paid, but you might be able to negotiate a settlement. This could depend on how long the debt has been outstanding, the amount of the original debt, and the motivation to settle the account.

Send the collection agency an unsolicited letter offering to settle the debt in exchange for removal of the negative information from the credit report. For example, you owe the original creditor $1,000 and the account is over 90 days past due. The creditor has charged off the amount as bad-debt and sold the debt to a collection agency. The agency paid $100 to buy the debt and plans to collect the entire $1,000 from you and make a $900 profit (these are estimates). Not a bad business model for a debt collector. The debt collector is running a business and owes you *nothing*, but he or she may be willing to settle the account for less than the $1,000 owed. If all you have is $300.... offer it in exchange for removal of the negative information from your credit report. Some debt negotiators suggest you offer as little as 7% of the outstanding amount and negotiate up from there if necessary. If the account is still with the original creditor you may have to offer a little more than you would propose to a 3rd party debt collector. You can still request to settle the account in exchange for removal of the negative information from your credit report.

Send the letter certified from the post office and use return receipt requested. If you call the collection agency on the phone and make arrangements you have no record of what was agreed to. The collection agency can say that you made a new agreement with them and your credit report can be updated with a *new* date of last date action extending the 7-year clock. Preserve your rights by paying the extra $2 at the post office for the green return receipt requested postcard. This provides documentation of any agreement between you and the collection agency. Someone at the collection agency has to sign for your letter when it arrives. The green card is mailed back to you and you now have proof of when your letter was received. I've included a sample request deletion letter.

Your Name
Your Address
City, State, Zip Code

Date

Creditor/Collection Agency Address
City, State, Zip

Re: Account #

Dear Sir or Madam:

I am writing in response to (your letter, phone call, the negative entry on my credit report) regarding (account number 123-456-789). I had some financial problems in the past that prevented me from addressing this issue but I am ready to resolve this matter now.

I never received any verification of the debt in accordance with the Fair Debt Collection Practices Act, and I am not acknowledging acceptance of the debt. I am currently negotiating with several creditors and I have a limited amount of funds to work with. I can only settle with those creditors that can satisfy the terms and conditions I am proposing.

Your company has the power to update this debt to the credit-reporting agency as you see fit, and I know you have the ability to change the negative entry since the information is provided by your agency. I am trying to re-establish my credit rating and need this negative entry removed. If you will assist me with this matter I can offer you some of the money I have available in exchange.

The amount I propose to pay towards full settlement of the debt is $_____. I am offering this amount in exchange for your agreement to delete and/or remove all information regarding this account on file with all of the credit reporting agencies.   If you accept this agreement please sign this letter of agreement and send me a copy. As soon as I receive it I will send certified payment in the amount of $_____.

I appreciate your willingness to work with me on saving us both time and effort.

Sincerely,

Your Name

If a creditor settles your debt and accepts a reduced payment you could still be liable for paying taxes on the amount forgiven. Creditors are supposed to notify the IRS for debt reductions of $600 or more, and the amount could be counted as taxable income, so check with your tax professional if you settle large debts.

Collection agencies are under *no obligation* to remove negative entries from your credit report. If they honor your request it is strictly as a courtesy to you. Be mindful of that when you approach them with this type of request. You can send a letter requesting deletion of an old account that was settled long ago. A Goodwill Letter requests that the negative account be removed from your credit report and is certainly worth a try. Having the negative item removed can positively impact your score. You can request a goodwill deletion of an entire account or of negative marks on a particular account. Include specifics about the month and year in which you are requesting a goodwill deletion for. Be polite and take the time to personalize the letter. Give the creditor 30 days to respond to your request.

Your Name
Your Address
Your City, State Zip

Date

Company Name
Company Address
City, State Zip

Re: Account Number

To Whom It May Concern:

I'm writing this letter to request your assistance in resolving a concern. A few years ago I suffered a time of financial crisis, I lost my job, got divorced, was ill. This event severely impacted my finances and I was unable to be on time with my payments on this account and take care of it in a timely manner as I had in the past. I was able to get current on the account listed above as soon as my finances improved, and I've enjoyed making timely payments since then. I've made the effort to make better, financial decisions and manage the credit I am privileged to receive much more responsibly.

I am in the process of buying a home, vehicle, starting a business, getting married, retiring, and I'm having difficulty receiving competitive interest rates due to the negative listing of this account on my credit report. I am kindly requesting that as an act of your goodwill, please remove this negative item from my credit report. I appreciate your kindness shown to me in this matter.

Sincerely,
Your Name

Some concerns can be resolved directly with the credit reporting agency. Use their suggested dispute initiation process. If the matter hasn't been successfully resolved through the online dispute process, you might be able to get help by speaking directly with a person at the credit reporting agency. Many consumers have problems with getting through to an actual human being at the different credit reporting agencies. Here are a few phone numbers, and instructions to get you through the voice prompts so that you can speak with a human being:

- Equifax 1-800-203-7843, Press 20 at each prompt, ignoring messages.
- Experian 1-800-493-1058, say "yes" when asked, enter credit report #, SS#, say "yes" again, say "agent", then "yes" to confirm.
- Transunion 1-800-916-8800, Press 2 at each prompt, ignoring messages.

There may be instances where you've tried and tried to resolve an issue with the credit-reporting agency to no avail. If you think you may have been treated unfairly you can file a complaint against the credit-reporting agency with the Federal Trade Commission. Follow the link below for more information:

https://www.ftccomplaintassistant.gov

You can also check out the website and possibly submit a complaint against creditors, or a credit reporting agency through the Consumer Finance Protection Board. Follow the link below to contact them for more information:

http://www.consumerfinance.gov/complaint/

Notes/Action Plan

Notes/Action Plan

Step 8: Raise Your Credit Score by Establishing Credit

Many people are leery of the credit card debt and avoid using credit cards entirely. A "cash only" policy might help to build wealth, but you'll need a credit history in order to keep preserve wealth. Unless you're paying 100% cash for a house or car, you'll need to obtain lender financing. Without a credit score you'll pay much higher interest rates (if you're able to obtain financing at all) which decreases wealth.

A good credit score is essential to secure the most competitive interest rates on mortgages, auto loans, and other types of lending. If you have a history of using cash exclusively you may find that you don't have a credit report or a credit score at all. To generate a credit score, the scoring model needs to compute a minimum criteria in order to rate the consumer. Ideally you should have at least one account open and reporting activity to the credit-reporting agency (CRA) within the last six months. This includes recent credit card use, or payments on an installment loan reporting to one of the three major CRAs.

Make sure your lenders report your activity to one or all three CRAs. Establishing a new account with a lender who doesn't report to the CRAs does little to improve your credit score. Ask the lender before you open the account (preferably before they check your credit score) if they report to one of the major CRAs. If you need to establish a credit history and the lender doesn't report your activity to a CRA, find another lender to work with.

Apply for a secured credit card to establish a credit history. The credit card laws of 2009 made it difficult for lenders to offer credit to young creditors who never had credit before, so a secured credit card is a great option for them. It's also an alternative for older people with limited credit histories, newly arrived immigrants to the U.S., and recent divorcees who need to establish credit on their own. The deposit you give the lender backs the secured credit card. Lenders require a minimum of $200 to open an account and issue a credit card. Some lenders

111

accept deposits up to about $5,000 but you don't have to deposit large amounts in order to get a card. Your deposit is placed in a money market deposit account. The creditor will send you a credit card with the Visa/MasterCard logo. The credit limit will be equal to the amount you have on deposit with the bank. Should you default on the account the bank will use the funds on deposit to pay off the credit card. Plan to keep the credit card long enough to start receiving unsecured credit card offers in the mail. The bank will return your deposit to you when you chose to close the account. It is practically a risk free transaction for the bank.

Find a card that offers the lowest interest rates and lowest annual fees. Remember to stay within the 20% utilization rate and use the credit card responsibly. You can charge as little as $1 or $5 per month to avoid becoming dependent on your credit card to make necessary purchases. Pay the bill promptly each month to generate activity on the account. If you are consistent, you may find after 9 months or so that creditors are sending offers for unsecured credit cards. Some secured card companies may offer to return your deposit and extend a line of credit to you as an unsecured account after a period of time.

There are several websites that let you comparison shop various points on secured credit cards:

www.bankrate.com
www.cardtrak.com
www.creditcards.com
www.nerdwallet.com

Another way to build a credit history is to get a gas card, or a retail account. These cards often have higher interest rates, but will extend credit limits of a few hundred dollars to people with limited credit histories. Again, be mindful of the 20% utilization rate when using department store cards because these cards are revolving accounts. The interest rates can be as high as 25% so you never want to carry a balance on these cards.

Any item you buy on sale in the store wouldn't be a bargain at all if you end up paying 25% interest on it.

A safe way to help a close friend or family member establish a credit history is to make him or her, an authorized user on one of your strongest revolving credit accounts. By making the person an authorized user you are "lending" them your credit history. This might be a more practical alternative to co-signing a loan for a friend or family member. If your credit is strong enough to be a co-signer, you should avoid taking on that risk for others. When you co-sign a loan for someone else, your credit rating is at the mercy of someone else's credit habits. If they're irresponsible, you'll have to step in and become primarily responsible for paying off the account, or you'll have to watch your credit score plummet. Use extreme caution when considering co-signing for anyone.

If you're the person who needs to establish a credit history, ask a trusted family member to make you an authorized user on one of their accounts. You want to be authorized on an account that is always paid as agreed, preferably one of their oldest accounts. Asking permission to use someone's money is hard so they may agree to make you an authorized user, yet not allow you the privilege of keeping the actual card. The advantage to being an authorized user is that every time the bank reports the most recent activity on that account to the CRA this information will also populate to your credit report. The account holder should be someone you trust with your financial history because as long as they pay their account on time you will benefit. However, if they *ever* decide to become irresponsible or miss a payment that negative information will *also* be reported to your credit report.

You don't have to use credit cards to build a credit history. Depending on your level of income and other factors you could apply for a personal line of credit or signature loan at a credit union or bank. Take out a signature loan (unsecured loan) for about $500 and *do not spend the money on anything.* In fact don't even leave the bank with the money. Immediately deposit the funds into a Money Market Deposit Account (MMDA), or a 6-month certificate of deposit (CD) at the same institution. You'll earn a little interest on the money you will have to pay interest on to borrow. Set up the account to make automatic payments to the signature loan each month. You will lose a few points because of the hard inquiry and the new amount of credit extended to you, but the bank will get their payments on time as agreed. This will provide consistent positive information to the credit-reporting agency which helps to increase your credit score.

Notes/Action Plan

Notes/Action Plan

Step 9: Raise Your Credit Score by Monitoring Your Credit

If you have a great credit score, pat yourself on the back! Only 13% of the US population has a score over 800. If you're not already in that 800+ club, there are things you can do to position yourself. You may not need to pay a costly monitoring service to help you monitor your credit as you improve it. Take advantage of the free credit reports available to you. Use the credit scores at www.creditsesame.com, www.creditkarma.com, and http://www.credit.com to monitor your credit score for free. You might not get a free FICO score, but the scores should be close enough to your FICO to detect any unusual activity.

Take advantage of the websites that offer free expert advice on improving your score. Observe the credit behaviors of high scorers and mimic what they do to get in that 800+ club. Stop wasting points on hard pulls. Inquiries cost too much to waste carelessly (12-20 points) so limit who you authorize to check your credit report. The average 720+ credit-score has about 2 inquires per year.

You can strategically comparison shop interest rates and other credit card terms using different websites. Keep your credit scores updated so you can compare Annual Percentage Rates (APRs) should you want to apply for credit. You can ask a lender for an informal quote based on the score that you pulled. Only work with creditors who indicate they will approve credit scores in your range and for the terms you want. This way you're not wasting hard inquiries. If the credit application doesn't strategically increase your credit position.... avoid it. The goal is to never *need* credit. Opt out of unsolicited credit card offers so that you decrease your risk of taking on unnecessary debt.

The credit card market is very competitive for customers with high credit scores. Card issuers offer anything from frequent flyer bonus miles, free hotel stays, and other kinds of lucrative reward deals just to get people to apply for their cards. Many people with high credit scores strategically use reward cards to save money and increase their credit position. A person with an 800 credit score, and supporting income requirements could apply for a new card just to get the 50,000 frequent flyer miles offered with the deal and take advantage of 1st class perks. After spending the minimum amounts required on the terms of agreement, they can close the card out and apply for a new card with additional perks the following year. Strategies like this only work for those who typically carry no balances on their credit cards.

People with high credit scores tend to pay off the balance in full before the due date. Opening a new account will still affect a high scorer but the recovery of points will be quicker. Having more credit available to use could increase your aggregate balance which looks good for credit utilization, and could increase your credit score. Be sure you are varying the types of credit applied for to get that strong mix of installment, revolving and mortgage credit.

Notes/Action Plan

Notes/Action Plan

Step 10: Raise Your Credit Score by Protecting Your Credit

If you have a high credit score you need to protect it. Anytime someone uses your name, social security number, credit card number, or other identifying info to buy things, open new accounts, or receive loans in your name it is identity theft. Recent studies have reported over 12 million victims of identity theft in the United States for the year 2012. The report released February 2013 by the Javelin Strategy & Research says that fraudsters stole over $21 billion, the highest amount since 2009. For more details on this report go to:

https://www.javelinstrategy.com/news/1387/92/1

18-24 is the most common age for victims of identity theft, but it can happen to anyone, at any age. The social security number is the most compromised identifier. Victimization frequently occurs close to home with friends and family being the main culprits. Monitor your credit reports often for early detection of identity theft.

If you've been a victim of identity theft, you can clean up your report but it's going to take some effort. File a police report on the fraudulent entries. Call the 800 numbers of three major credit-reporting agencies to place a fraud alert on your credit report:

- Equifax (800) 525-6285
- Experian (888) 397-3742
- TransUnion (800) 680-7289

A fraud alert notifies lenders to follow certain procedures before they open new accounts in your name or make changes to existing accounts. The initial fraud alert lasts for 90 days. Contact one credit reporting agency (CRA) and they will place the alert on the other two credit reports. This is the only time the three major CRAs work together (besides when they give you that free annual report once per year). When you place the fraud alert, you can get another free copy of your credit report.

If any fraudulent accounts were opened or any of your existing accounts were tampered with, contact the lenders and close those accounts immediately. Contact all the creditors involved, and cancel all credit and bankcards involved in the identity theft. Lenders may require a copy of the police report, and reports to the CRAs in order to discharge the debt. You can also file a complaint with the Federal Trade Commission and fill out an ID Theft Affidavit:

http://www.ftc.gov/opa/2002/02/idtheft.shtm

For more information call or write:

877-438-4338, TTY 1-866-653-4261
Identity Theft Clearinghouse
Federal Trade Commission
Washington, DC 20580

Some of the highest credit scores I've ever seen have belonged to people who were formerly victims of identity theft. The experience made them hyper vigilant about monitoring and using their credit, which caused their credit scores to rise higher than they were before they were victimized. It will take some work to recover but it can be done.

There are things you can do to protect yourself against identity theft. Keep personal data private by using stronger password protection, shredding documents, and monitoring your accounts. Ensure there is bank-level security encryption when conducting online transaction. Seriously consider all data security breaches and above all, do not delay in reporting identity theft.

Copy the front and back of every credit card, bankcard, and store card in your possession. Keep copies of the cards in a locked file, or a safety deposit box. Should your security be compromised you can immediately contact all the creditors. You'll be able to quickly reference the account numbers using the copies and cancel these credit cards. You can also use those copies when paying down debt and you need to cut up cards, yet leave the accounts open.

Active duty service members can place an active duty fraud alert on their credit report as a precaution for up to a year. Service members are most susceptible to identity theft when they are deployed and unable to monitor credit reports and mail. The fraud alert tells a lender to take certain steps to verify the identity of the credit applicant. As with identity theft, if you call one CRA to place an active duty fraud alert on your report, they are required to notify the other two agencies.

While taking action to increase your credit scores, you'll want to closely monitor your credit report. Check monthly to ensure that changes are being implemented, and to detect any unusual activity. When identity thieves open accounts to steal goods and services in your name, they typically re-direct the bills to somewhere other than your address. The consumer never receives a bill until the account becomes way past due and goes to collection. The collection agency works to locate the consumer and by the time the consumer learns of the account, these bills have gone unpaid for some time.

If you have a relatively high score, you should freeze your credit reports as a form of protection. A security freeze prevents thieves from opening new accounts in your name. 49 states and the District of Columbia have enacted laws to help consumers protect their credit identity, and a credit security freeze is one of the strongest forms of protection. Law enforcement agencies, insurance companies and creditors that already have an established relationship with you may still be able to view your report, but a freeze limits the unsolicited viewing of your report. It restricts anyone from obtaining instant credit in your name, essentially *locking* up your credit files.

Once you enact a security freeze, you can temporarily lift the freeze in order to access new credit or review your own credit history. The consumer has to unlock the credit file to authorize an inquiry using a special PIN number provided by the CRA. There is normally no charge to place a security freeze; however some states require a small fee to lift the security freeze temporarily or permanently. To refinance a home, purchase a new vehicle, or allow a potential employer to check your credit as part of a background check, temporarily lift the freeze for a specified period of time (a week to 30 days). A credit freeze can be cost effective over the long run if you have a good credit score and don't plan to seek new credit for a year or more. You can enact the freeze and have peace of mind knowing that access to new credit applications is restricted without your permission.

The 49 states and the District of Columbia provide this protection to consumers suggest you contact each CRA directly to enact the request. You can find frequently asked questions and determine if a credit security freeze is the right decision for you at:

http://defendyourdollars.org/document/guide-to-security-freeze-protection

Place a credit security freeze on your credit report within the state that you pay your bills. The following states offer instructions on placing the freeze as well as sample request letters to send to each CRA.

Alaska: http://consumersunion.org/wp-content/uploads/2013/04/securityAK.pdf

Arizona: http://consumersunion.org/wp-content/uploads/2013/04/securityAZ.pdf

Arkansas: http://consumersunion.org/wp-content/uploads/2013/04/securityAR.pdf

California: http://www.oag.ca.gov/idtheft/facts/freeze-your-credit

Colorado: http://consumersunion.org/wp-content/uploads/2013/04/securityCO.pdf

Connecticut: http://consumersunion.org/wp-content/uploads/2013/04/securityCO.pdf

Delaware: http://consumersunion.org/wp-content/uploads/2013/04/securityDE.pdf

District of Columbia: http://consumersunion.org/wp-content/uploads/2013/04/securityDC.pdf

Florida: http://consumersunion.org/wp-content/uploads/2013/04/securityFL.pdf

Georgia: http://consumer.georgia.gov/consumer-topics/credit-freeze

Hawaii: http://consumersunion.org/wp-content/uploads/2013/04/securityHI.pdf

Idaho: http://consumersunion.org/wp-content/uploads/2013/04/securityID.pdf

Indiana: http://consumersunion.org/wp-content/uploads/2013/04/securityIN.pdf

Illinois: http://consumersunion.org/wp-content/uploads/2013/04/securityIL.pdf

Iowa: http://consumersunion.org/wp-content/uploads/2013/04/securityIA.pdf

Kansas: http://consumersunion.org/wp-content/uploads/2013/04/securityKS.pdf

Kentucky: http://consumersunion.org/wp-content/uploads/2013/04/securityKY.pdf

Louisiana: http://www.ag.state.la.us/Shared/ViewDoc.aspx?Type=2&Doc=113

125

Maine: http://consumersunion.org/wp-content/uploads/2013/04/securityME.pdf

Maryland: http://consumersunion.org/wp-content/uploads/2013/04/securityMD.pdf

Massachusetts: http://consumersunion.org/wp-content/uploads/2013/04/securityMA.pdf

Minnesota: http://consumersunion.org/wp-content/uploads/2013/04/securityMN.pdf

Mississippi: http://consumersunion.org/wp-content/uploads/2013/04/securityMS.pdf

Missouri: http://consumersunion.org/wp-content/uploads/2013/04/securityMO.pdf

Montana: http://consumersunion.org/wp-content/uploads/2013/04/securityMT.pdf

Nebraska: http://consumersunion.org/wp-content/uploads/2013/04/securityNE.pdf

Nevada: http://consumersunion.org/wp-content/uploads/2013/04/securityNV.pdf

New Hampshire: http://doj.nh.gov/consumer/identity-theft/documents/sample-security-freeze.pdf

New Jersey: http://www.state.nj.us/oag/ca/brief/securityfreeze.pdf

New Mexico: http://consumersunion.org/wp-content/uploads/2013/04/securityNM.pdf

New York: http://www.nyc.gov/html/ofe/html/protect/alert.shtml

North Carolina: http://www.ncdoj.com/Protect-Yourself/2-4-3-Protect-Your-Identity/Protect-Yourself/Freeze-Your-Credit.aspx

North Dakota: http://consumersunion.org/wp-content/uploads/2013/04/securityND.pdf

Ohio: http://consumersunion.org/wp-content/uploads/2013/04/securityOH.pdf

Oklahoma: http://consumersunion.org/wp-content/uploads/2013/04/securityOK.pdf

Oregon: http://consumersunion.org/wp-content/uploads/2013/04/securityOR.pdf

Pennsylvania: http://consumersunion.org/wp-content/uploads/2013/04/securityPA.pdf

Rhode Island: http://consumersunion.org/wp-content/uploads/2013/04/securityRI.pdf

South Carolina: http://consumersunion.org/wp-content/uploads/2013/04/securitySC.pdf

South Dakota: http://consumersunion.org/wp-content/uploads/2013/04/securitySD.pdf

Tennessee: http://consumersunion.org/wp-content/uploads/2013/04/securityTN.pdf

Texas: http://consumersunion.org/wp-content/uploads/2013/04/securityTN.pdf

Utah: http://consumersunion.org/wp-content/uploads/2013/04/securityUT.pdf

Virginia: http://consumersunion.org/wp-content/uploads/2013/04/securityVA.pdf

Vermont: http://consumersunion.org/wp-content/uploads/2013/04/securityVT.pdf

Washington: http://www.atg.wa.gov/ConsumerIssues/ID-Privacy/SecurityFreeze.aspx

West Virginia: http://consumersunion.org/wp-content/uploads/2013/04/securityWV.pdf

Wisconsin: http://consumersunion.org/wp-content/uploads/2013/04/securityWI.pdf

Wyoming: http://consumersunion.org/wp-content/uploads/2013/04/securityWY.pdf

Keep in mind, the three major CRAs exist to gather and compile information about consumers, which they then sell to businesses with a legitimate business interest. Creditors and insurance companies review these files to determine if they will offer you their product. You can choose not to receive prescreened offers from credit card and insurance companies for five years, or choose to opt-out permanently. The three major CRA's have provided a phone number and website where you can opt out.

To opt out for 5 years: Call 1-888-5-OPT-OUT (1-888-567-8688) or go to www.optoutprescreen.com

To opt our permanently: Begin the process online at www.optoutprescreen.com. You can print out and sign the Permanent Opt-Out Election Form.

During this process you will be asked to provide personal information which is used for verification purposes and kept confidential. If you'd like to handle this request by mail, send a written request to each CRA. Here's a sample letter to send to all of the major CRA's.

Your Name
Your Address
Your City, State Zip

Date

CRA Name
Address
City, State Zip

To Whom It May Concern:

I am requesting that you remove my name from your marketing lists. I know that you are bound, as per state/federal laws, to remove my name from your mailing lists upon request. I also know that you cannot send me any mail without my prior approval.

I am including the following information you have asked for to process my request:

Full Name:
Current Mailing Address:
Previous Mailing Address:
Social Security Number:
Date of Birth:

Thank you in advance for your prompt handling of this request.

Sincerely,

Your Name

Send the letter to one of the major CRA's listed below:

Experian
Opt Out
P.O. Box 919
Allen, Texas 75013

TransUnion
Name Removal Option
P.O. Box 505
Woodlyn, PA 19094

Equifax
Options
P.O. Box 740123
Atlanta, Georgia 30374

Innovis Consumer Assistance
P.O. Box 495
Pittsburgh, PA 15230

While credit scores may seem impossible to control, it is my hope that this work has inspired you to do the work to raise your credit score. If you already enjoy good credit, I hope the strategies will help you maximize your score and continue to enjoy all the advantages that come with a high credit score. Practice aggressive credit score management and guard your credit score. It can save you hundreds to thousands of dollars and impact your overall personal financial management.

Raise *Your Credit Score in 10 Easy Steps* is the 1st title released in *The Create Your Money Series*. Each title deals specifically with financial topics and information that motivates wealth creation. My books are designed to be quick-reads.... I'm giving you the streamlined, absolutely essential information you need to know, in order to create the money you want, and change your life. I wish you *complete* success on your journey to improved credit scores, lower interest rates, more competitive credit offers, and more money in your pocket!

Before you go, I want to thank you for taking the time to buy and read my book. There are dozens of other personal finance books you could have chosen, but you took a chance on me. I'm thrilled that you read this book all the way to the end and I hope that you got a lot out of it. If you liked what you've read then I need your help.... please take a moment to leave a review for this book on Amazon.

Your feedback helps me to continue writing the kind of books that help you create your money and change your world. If you think this information is worth sharing, please take a few seconds to tell your friends on Facebook and Twitter. If it helps them keep more money in their pocket they'll be grateful to you and so will I!

Click on the link below to leave feedback:

http://www.amazon.com/Raise-Credit-Create-Series-ebook/dp/B00CQUW8QQ/ref=sr_1_1?ie=UTF8&qid=137218615 7&sr=8-1&keywords=angel+love+credit+scores

Visit my website at:

www.AngelLoveCreateYourMoney.com

https://www.facebook.com/AngelLoveCreateYourMoney?ref=stream

@AngelLoveCreate

Notes/Action Plan

40378442R00078

Made in the USA
Lexington, KY
03 April 2015